THE EASTMAN EXPLOSION TRAGEDY

DARK DAY IN OCTOBER, 1960

On a beautiful autumn day in October, 1960, the peaceful skies around Kingsport, Tennessee, were suddenly rent with a tremendous blast, sending vibrations that shattered plate glass windows and rocked buildings throughout the 35,000 residents of the city.

Something had exploded, but what?

The industrial city of Kingsport had several facilities where some sort of detonation could have occurred.

A large mushroom-like cloud arose in the Southeast sky from downtown, in the direction of several local plants, including Metrogas, Blue Ridge Glass Manufacturers, and Tennessee Eastman's sprawling complex of plants and buildings.

All over the city, plate glass and other windows broke, walls were damaged, and plaster cracked.

Immediately suspect was Metrogas, but observers quickly learned that the horrifying blast came from one of the large Eastman plants.

The ultra modern, 3 year old Aniline Plant had suddenly exploded, wreaking death and destruction through other near by buildings and parking areas.

Fires broke out, steel beams, brick and other debris flew through the air for thousands of feet.

Sirens wailed, huge storage tanks of deadly chemicals exploded, 55 gal. drums of stored material erupted in blasts that echoed through shattered walls.

In this most deadly explosion at Tennessee's largest manufacturing plant, deaths and destruction would mar the beauty of the October day, and firemen, workmen and officers would work through the entire night, attempting to recover bodies and rescue the injured.

The Aniline Plant, only 3 years old, was supposed to be super safe and secure from such occurrence.

In the confused and desperate hours following the blast, gruesome discoveries were made. Arms, legs, hands, bodies were found, damaged vehicles and other property amounted to almost more than could be counted.

Seventeen men died in the blast, others would never fully recover from injuries or shock sustained.

Since the establishment of Tennessee Eastman in the early part of 1920, this was the most deadly industrial accident recorded.

And even today, some survivors wonder why it happened.

THE EASTMAN EXPLOSION TRAGEDY

By Pete Dykes

Many decades have passed since that fateful October in 1960 when Kingsport was rocked and shocked by a tremendous explosion at one of the Tennessee Eastman Company plants.

Death and destruction struck suddenly and unexpectedly, leaving a stunned and grieving population in their wake.

The memory of that horrifying day is yet fresh and vivid in the minds of many of those who lived through it.

In this account of the tragedy we will relate personal accounts of the tragedy by several other individuals. We also have included letters from readers who remember the fateful explosion.

October 4, 1960

Chapter 1

Kermit Young's ad was going to be late again. I knew I would get chewed out by Charlie Hamlet, the big, white-haired composing room foreman, when I turned it in.

He'd probably complain to Ben Haden, who was now General Manager of the newspaper, partly because he knew a little bit about the business and mostly because his father-in-law, C. P. Edwards, owned the place. Well, at nearly three hundred bucks a page, the double-truck ad would justify being a bit late, I figured. Hardly anyone ever gets fired for bringing in too much business, even if it is later than it should be.

For ten years now, I had been working in the advertising department at the Times. Jack Huffaker, who was Advertising Manager for most of that time, had sort of trained me to take over the big grocery store accounts, Oakwood Markets, owned by Dick Stout and Wallace Boyd, Cut Rate Food Stores, owned by the LeGuardias, and The Little Store, Kermit's own little gold mine. I didn't have any problem with Oakwood, Dale Simpson, manager of the Sullivan Street store, always had the ad made up and ready on time. Cut Rate was a jewel. Tommy Davis, their advertising man, always made up the ad and brought it to the newspaper for me, so all I had to do was make out an order form and send it upstairs on the dumbwaiter. But Kermit's ads were entirely another matter.

He was always late, and often...uh...incapacitated. He'd call me at my home at eleven o'clock at night, sometimes, and beg me to come to his Watauga Street home and finish up his ad for him and get it to the newspaper sometime during the night shift. Like a sap, I did it, too. Kermit would have his ad partly made up, spread all over the dining room table, with bits and pieces of paper all over, some of them stuck on the sides of the layout like little flags, on which he had scribbled items and prices he had forgotten to put in where they were supposed to go.

He would, of course, be somewhat in his cups, but determined to get the ad finished in time to get it in the newspaper and pull in customers.

He knew how to do it, too, darn him. He might have had a problem with the temperance society, but he was one of the best grocery store promoters I have ever known.

This day, a Tuesday, was deadline for Thursday advertising. The other accounts were all already in the shop, but there I sat, across the cluttered desk in Kermit's tiny upstairs office, waiting for Doyle Gilliam to finish up putting a few last minute price changes down.

Kermit was out of town, but he had trained Doyle, his manager, to do the ads the same way HE did them. . .always late.

Deadline was supposed to be three o'clock, but I had reserved space with the "dummy" girl, and had notified John, the "dispatcher" that the ad was on the way. All I had to do now was get Doyle to turn it loose so I could take it back to my desk and paste the order, which I had already written up, on top, and send it to be typeset.

"That'll do it," Doyle said, rolling up the clumsy double page spread and handing it across the desk to me.

"Sorry I'm late, but Mr. Young called and told me to be sure and get these late prices in."

"OK, Doyle," I said. "I'll get it in and…"

Just at that moment, the building shook as if it had been struck by something.

"Gosh!" I exclaimed. "A car's run in to the store!"

"Felt like it," Doyle said.

We ran out of the little office and down the narrow stairs to the hidden door beside the bakery counter.

Pushing through the big glass doors, we hurried outside.

There was no car, no wreck, no sign of damage.

"Daggone!" Doyle said. "We sure felt somethin'. Could that have been an earthquake?"

"I don't know," I replied. "Could have been something like that."

I went to my car and headed back toward the newspaper.

Chapter 2

From the Little Store parking lot, I turned down Clay Street and drove across Center to Market.

In the downtown area, still on Market Street, I began to notice shattered plate glass windows.

At Charles Stores, corner of Broad and Market, a big window was broken out, and there were several others in like condition along the street.

In the distant sky, toward the East, a large dust cloud seemed to be rising.

At the newspaper advertising office, on the street floor on Market Street, the big front plate glass window was shattered completely out, broken bits of glass shards all over the pavement and the inside lobby floor.

Paul Wallen and Charles Sigman, the Classified boys, were crawling out from under desks, where they had hidden when the sudden blast scared them out of two years growth. Wade Young was trying to get out from under his own desk, but was stuck, and was grunting and pushing, trying to get his bulk out of the knee-hole space that was never designed to hold so much matter.

The dummy girl was white as a sheet, standing at the back of the room beside Maurice William's desk. Maurice was setting at his desk, not a hair out of place, as usual, shuffling papers as if he was doing something, which he was, if you consider shuffling papers a thing to do

"What happened?" I asked.

"We don't know," Sigman said. "There was a man standing here at the counter, placing an ad. All at once, the window blew up. He jumped all the way over the counter! We dived under desks, thought a bomb had gone off. The girls were upstairs. What happened, anyway?"

"My gosh," I said. "It must have been the gas plant. It must have blown up!"

I handed the rolled up ad to the dummy girl and asked her to send it up to dispatch.

"The order's on my desk," I told her, "I'm going to go find out what happened."

Running across the street to my car, I jumped in and started up Market Street, in the direction of the giant dust cloud I could see in the distance.

Metro Gas, a bottled gas plant, was situated beside the American St. Gobain Glass Plant on the old highway that ran through the Eastman property and Long Island.

My wife had worked at St. Gobain some years earlier, and we had a number of friends still employed there.

The dust cloud, ominous in the sky, loomed ahead. At the railroad underpass on Wilcox Drive, I could see the flames and dust cloud more clearly. It sure looked like it was at the Gas Plant.

There was no traffic, no cars nor trucks moving at all on the highway.

I parked my car at an abandoned gasoline station at the end of Sullivan Street and ran afoot through the underpass.

Along Lincoln Street, a narrow sidewalk runs all the way to what once was called "Edgewood Village" and is now more Eastman property or city roadways.

I could see the big dust cloud better now, and there were flames and flashes of light reflecting in it.

I ran up the sidewalk, hoping to get close enough to find out what had happened, so I could get back to the newspaper office with the information.

I could see the gas plant. It was not on fire, and there had been no explosion there.

Sirens began wailing, and a fire truck raced past me, heading up Lincoln Street.

At the Glass Plant gates, just across the railroad siding tracks, a crowd of men began pouring out just as I ran up.

"Lemme out of here" I heard one of them yell.

"What happened?" I hollered at them.

"Hell, we don't know," one man yelled back. "Everything just blew up. People dead all over the place. We climbed over the fence and got out of there."

"Is it the glass plant?" I yelled.

"Hell, no!" he yelled back. "It's the Eastman. And if the rest of it goes up, this whole place is going with it!"

Chapter 3

Ambulances and fire trucks were racing past now, heading toward the Edgewood entrance of the Eastman Plant.

I turned and ran back down the street to my car, and hurried back to the newspaper office.

The staff there had already found out part of what had happened, and where the explosion had taken place.

There had been calls from Paris, France; London, England and Rome, Italy, inquiring what the explosion was, for it had set off seismograph needles all over the world, sending them racing around the dials in a frenzy that confused and shocked the people watching them.

So many local calls had come in, the switchboard was jammed, and reporters and photographers were heading toward their cars to go out and cover the disaster.

I immediately thought of my wife and children at home, and began to worry about their safety. The switchboard was still jammed, and there was no way to telephone home to find out what the situation might be there.

"I think I'll go home to check on things,"

"Wait a minute, Pete," Ben Haden called to me.

"We may need you to do some art work or something on this thing. We don't know what kind of pictures we might be able to get."

"I'll be back in thirty minutes," I told him.

"That should do her," he replied.

I ran to my car and drove home. My wife was at the door, our two little boys, ages 7 and 9, crowded beside her.

"We were worried about you," she said. "Our telephone seems to be working, but we couldn't get any answer at the paper."

I explained about the jammed switchboard.

There had already been news flashes on the radio, with as much information as I had. By the time I got back to the newspaper office, reporters had already been to the scene and the first of them were already back, working up stories for a special edition, if needed.

Charlie Houser, the Pressroom foreman, had waited around, knowing the night crew would not come to work until late that night. He and A. B. Akard, his second in command, were ready to print a special run if Haden decided to go with it.

When a big news story breaks, a newsroom, even on a small newspaper, is a mighty busy place. Reporters typed furiously, re-write editors grabbed their copy and hammered it in to better shape, hurrying down to the composing room with the long sheets of copy paper.

Photographers came running in, heading for the photo lab, which was churning out negatives and quick, wet photo prints as rapidly as humanly possible.

The telephones were all working now, and just about every person in the place had a desk phone propped between shoulder and ear, talking while they typed or wrote.

I hung around long enough to make sure I wouldn't be needed for retouching or other art work, then told Ben I was going home.

He nodded, not missing a word of the telephone conversation he was having with someone.

Outside the crisp October evening air felt welcome, cool and calm after the excited atmosphere in the newsroom.

Sirens were still wailing in the distance, as over-worked ambulances transported the injured, maimed and dying to Holston Valley Community Hospital. Police, Firemen and volunteer citizens were at each street intersection, directing the rushing flow of traffic.

It was going to be a long, long night.

Chapter 4

The 40 year old plant known locally as TEC had constantly undergone revamps and new construction, keeping pace with modern improvements and facilities.

An offshoot of Kodak, the camera and photographic film manufacturer based in Rochester, New York and founded by George Eastman (1854-1932) the Tennessee plant had become a highly diversified facility, producing a variety of chemicals and products.

Kodak, a multinational corporation, had dominated the film market and led the way in mass production of inexpensive and simple cameras.

Eastman's first camera model was sold pre-loaded with film, and after the purchaser snapped the photos, he mailed the entire camera back to Rochester, where the film was removed, the pictures printed, new film loaded, and the whole thing sent back to the customer for another bout of picture taking.

Over the years, roll film had been developed and cameras simplified, enabling local or area film processors to develop the film and print photos.

In the earlier days, production of film was the key to Kodak's huge profits. When World War I disrupted the German supply of photographic paper, optical glass, gelatin and an assortment of chemicals including methanol, acetic acid and acetone, Kodak faced a serious problem.

Knowing the forests of the Appalachian South could provide a great source of raw materials for the manufacture of methanol and acetone, Kodak became immediately interested in 1920 when approached by officials of the Clinchfield Railroad and representatives of the Kingsport Improvement Company, developers of the planned industrial community.

George Eastman visited East Tennessee in July of 1920 and purchased 35 acres and the factory buildings of a government owned wood alcohol plant, constructed as a part of the war effort but never operated. It was known as the American Wood Reduction Company. Eastman expanded his original purchase to include an additional three hundred acres for a total investment of more than a million dollars, a considerable sum in 1920.

Because innately everything was manufactured from wood, a renewable source, Eastman bought up timber rights for miles around and even built a "dinky" railroad out to Blairs Gap to haul logs to their giant saw mill.

J. C. White, who was later to become president of Tennessee Eastman, came to Kingsport with his father to operate the big saw mill. Lumber, wood alcohol, methanol, charcoal, acetic acid, hardwood pitch and wood preserving oil were some of the products originally produced at the Tennessee plant.

During the mid 1920s two developments of significance shaped the company's direction. The demands for safety film for home movies and the need for X-ray film coincided with the successful research of Eastman chemists and resulted in the production of acetic anhydride from pyroligneous acid, one of the primary ingredients used in manufacturing cellulose acetate, the base for safety film.

Cellulose acetate production was transferred from Kodak Park in New York to TEC in 1929. That same year, TEC began production of acetic anhydride and in 1930, began to develop cellulose acetate yarn, which was being produced on a large scale within a year.

Soon TEC began production of Tenite cellulosic plastics, acetate dyestuffs, as well as Tenite II, a cellulose acetate butyrate molding composition. In 1930, Kodak transferred the manufacture of hydroquinone from Passaic Junction, New Jersey, to Kingsport. By 1940, annual sales had reached nearly $29 million.

When World War II halted the availability of natural rubber supplies from Asia, the Allies developed a commercial method for making synthetic rubber based on a process that depended on hydroquinone. As a result, TEC developed a close relationship with the War Production Board. In 1941, the National Defense Research Committee (NDRC) contacted TEC's general manager James C. White and requested that a pilot plant be initiated for the manufacture of the powerful explosive called RDX.

The highly volatile explosive was desperately needed in the war against Nazi submarines, who were sinking Allied ships at an alarming rate.

H. G. "Herb" Stone (1897-1976) led the effort to develop RDX and served as works manager of the Holston Ordnance Works. Soon TEC was manufacturing RDX and Composition B in large quantities needed to win the war in the European theatre. In June, 1942, TEC received official authorization from the U.S. Army Ordnance and NDRC to design and operate Holston Ordnance Works (HOW). Subsequently HOW became the world's largest manufacturer of high explosives, and received the prestigious Army-Navy "E" Award for "outstanding achievement in the production of material of war".

Scientists from TEC were heavily involved in the Manhattan Project at Oak Ridge, which led to the development of the atomic bomb which ended the war.

By the 1950s, acetate yarn became TEC's major product, with annual sales of $130 million. During all these years, the plants had operated with an excellent degree of safety, although minor explosions and other difficulties sometimes occurred in those areas where chemicals were produced.

Although Tennessee Eastman was the most successful Industrial development in Kingsport, the city's first effort in that direction brought an earlier chemical plant, the Federal Dyestuff and Chemical Corporation plant to the banks of the Holston River some fifteen years before George Eastman purchased what was to become the TEC property.

In October, 1915, the Federal Dyestuff and Chemical Corporation was incorporated in Delaware with an impressive capitalization of fifteen million dollars, a tremendous amount in that year.

Curtailment of the import of dyestuffs from Germany during World War I and the need for military explosives were the major factors in launching this venture.

Government statistics showed that fifty million pounds of dyestuffs had been imported in 1913, but very little during the next two years.

Congress passed a law placing a protective duty on dyestuffs to encourage domestic manufacture as quickly as possible.

Rockefeller and du Pont powder interests were believed to be the principal investors.

The company acquired 200 acres of land in Kingsport, bordering the Holston River and served by the recently completed Carolina, Clinchfield and Ohio Railroad.

Ambitious plans included production of dyestuffs, pharmaceuticals and even inorganic chemicals such as barium choloide and blanc fixe. Construction began in 1915 and by the end of 1916, the company had erected twenty nine buildings for the prodcution of chemicals, intermediates and dyestuffs.

Except for Fredrick Ross' ill-fated silk mill venture nearly a half century earlier, this was the first industrial development in Kingsport.

The plant site was strategically located for the supply of basic raw materials for coal tar dyes: coal, sulfur, and salt.

Soon after opening, the plant was producing caustic soda, chlorine, sodium, hydrochloric acid and nitric acid. Daily capacity of hydrochloric acid alone was 40,000 pounds.

Labor conditions were very favorable, as Eastman would find them to be a few years later.

Because the city of Kingsport was underdeveloped at the time, the company built its own guest house for visitors, a two story building with sleeping porches, which was also used as a clubhouse for entertaining executives. The plant's first shipment of dyes was made to a Hosiery Mill in Riverside, New Jersey, and soon railcar shipments were being sent out.

In addition to the dyes, by November 1916, the plant had produced 800,000 pounds of explosives. Some 50,000 pounds of chemicals and dyestuffs were being produced daily and plans were made to double that output by 1917.

The first explosion known to happen at the plant took place on February 19, 1916, and set fire to a chemical tank, but employees were able to prevent the flames from spreading and only one building was damaged.

But on May 7, 1917, an explosion in the munitions area killed one employee and burned two others severely, resulting in their later deaths. Sabotage was suspected, although federal troops had been acting as guards for the facility. Hoping to gain additional investors and expand, an annual profit of more than $2 million was estimated in a prospectus to sell stock. Even higher profits were predicted for 1917; but the end of the war brought a sudden decline in sales to the army, and the expansion bubble burst.

In October 1917, the company went into receivership and the assets of Federal Dyestuff an Chemical were sold to Union Dye and Chemical Company for $1 million, operating until 1921, when that firm went bankrupt.

A portion of the "Dye Plant" property became part of what was to become TEC.

Chapter 5

No one who lived through that night of the Eastman explosion will ever forget it.

Billy R. Burgan of Mt. Carmel, certainly won't:

"I had just finished working the 6:30 am to 3 p.m. shift at American Saint Gobain (now AFG) which is next door to Eastman.

I live in Mt. Carmel, but I needed to go through town and pick up some cleaning on Island Street. As I started to pay for my cleaning, I heard a loud "boom" and jumped as the plate glass window fell in behind me. My thought was that a jet plane had flown over, broken the sound barrier and the vibrations had caused the window to shatter. The glass breaking did not bother me because I had experienced broken glass piling up around me and others many times over the years of working at the glass plant.

I was really glad I was not scared because the cashier became very frightened and nervous...the bill for my cleaning was $3.50, I gave her a five dollar bill and she gave back a twenty-dollar bill, a five, a ten, four ones and 50 cents in change. I told her she had given me back too much money, but she was so shaky she just said, 'pay me what you owe me and I'll put it all back in the cash register.'

As I came back out onto the street, I looked over toward Eastman and saw a large column of smoke rolling upward in the sky. It was then I realized there must have been an explosion either at Eastman or the glass plant. I began to get a little nervous because I was chief operator on a production line and we used propane gas and oxygen on the line. We had storage tanks out behind the plant and it was my responsibility to turn the valves off on these tanks at the end of the shift. The question of whether I had turned the valves off kept running through my mind.

I hurriedly jumped into my car to go see where and find out what had happened.

As soon as I got into the car I turned on my CB radio and heard two men talking about all the smoke and where it was originating from. I broke in on their conversation to find out if they had a fix on it. One of the men said he was on Cherry Hill in West View and could see all over Kingsport and it looked like it was coming from behind the glass plant.

It was then I almost panicked, because I thought I might be responsible for this disaster. As I sat in my car trying to calm down, I heard the man on the CB say that the smoke had cleared enough to determine that it was not coming from the glass plant. He also said there had been a terrible explosion at Eastman, just across the fence from the glass plant. Although I was somewhat relieved to know it was not the propane and oxygen tanks at the glass plant, I feared there would be many casualties as a result of the explosion.

By this time, the news of the explosion was on the radio and TV, so I thought it best to go on home. The sound of all the sirens from the emergency vehicles and the police units made my hair stand on end. When I got home, my wife and neighbors were standing in the yard waiting for me and praying that I had not been hurt since this had happened so close to where I worked.

As the hours passed and we learned of all those who had lost their lives and of the many who had been injured in the explosion, I knew I had so much for which I needed to thank God. I am sure that this is one day that is deeply embedded in the memory of all of us who lived here when this terrible tragedy happened. My thoughts and prayers still go out to those families who lost so much on that October day."

Chapter 6

Joan Lamberson, Kingsport, had just arrived home that October day, when she heard the blast and decided to go to the hospital, where she worked as a volunteer. Traffic in the area was very heavy, and upon arrival at the hospital she found the halls full of people, both blast victims trying to get word to their families that they were alive, and family members trying to locate and find out the condition of their loved ones.

Lamberson spent long hours aiding the blast victims and vividly remembers going to the aid of one man in the hall who was covered in blood and going into shock.

Civil defense workers were in her neighborhood, only a few blocks from the explosion, when she arrived home very late. Her family had refused to be evacuated until she arrived.

Her best and worst memories of the event are the horrible day and night of hearing the details of the lives lost and injuries suffered and the quick action and community spirit and cooperation that saved many lives and comforted grieving families.

Freddie A. Shepherd, now living in Rutledge, TN, has these memories of that day:

"I had worked the 'graveyard' shift in Eastman's CE Division Analytical Laboratory on October 3, and after getting off work at 7:00 a.m. October 4, had slept until about 3:30 that afternoon.

Sometime around 4:30 I had gone out in our front yard at 1625 East Sevier Avenue to do some yard work and talk to my wife and a friend who were sitting on the steps of our front porch.

Just minutes before the explosion our friend had taken her infant daughter who had been in a stroller on the sidewalk by the steps, and left to go back to her home on Carolina Avenue.

My wife had just gotten up and gone inside and I had walked over to our driveway, about ten steps from the porch when I heard a sound like the sharp crack and pinging whistle that a 90 mm tank gun would make.

What in the world is going on – who is shooting around here, I remember thinking, and looking up toward where the sound came from, I saw dust and smoke coming out of the windows on the South end of the J. P. Stevens plant.

Before I had time to move or react there was the loudest explosion I had every heard, and our front glass storm door was blown apart, with glass flying all over the porch and walk where my wife and our friend and her daughter had been sitting just minutes before."

Chapter 7

Freddie Shepherd's account continues

I was still looking at the J. P. Stevens building when all this happened and it looked like the whole end was being torn off. Of course it wasn't, just a lot of dust and dirt flying around from the force of the explosion at Eastman's Aniline plant, but I didn't know that yet. I thought J. P. Stevens had blown up.

Several days later I got to thinking about what I had heard and figured that the first sounds I heard must have been the initial sounds from the blast. We also found out later that a piece of debris from the explosion had gone through a picture window, landing in the living room floor of a house just a couple of houses down the street from us.

I ran into the house, not knowing what I would find because of the storm door being blown apart. However, that door was the only apparent damage, and after seeing that my wife was OK, I told her that J. P. Stevens had blown up and I was going down the road to see if I could find out more about what had happened.

I ran down East Sevier to the corner, turned right, and ran down Eastman Road to the bridge over the railroad. I saw that it was not J. P. Stevens, but something at Eastman.

Looking down on the site from the bridge was like looking at a war scene. Torn up buildings, fire everywhere, more explosions throwing debris in the air, people running in every direction, and stuff still falling out of the air all around me.

Just then a man came running up the bridge from the direction of the explosion. He had blood all over his face from a deep cut just over his right eye, and he stopped and asked me how bad did it look like he was hurt. I helped him get the bleeding stopped and told him it looked like he only had one cut, but it would need several stitches.

He said that he had been walking to his car when it happened and didn't know what had hit him, but he knew that he was hurt and took off running to get as far away from there as possible. Then, while holding a handkerchief over the cut, he glanced back down toward the plant and said "there are a bunch of people hurt real bad down there, I'll be alright" and started walking on down the road away from the explosion.

I went back home and told my wife that something at Eastman had blown up and it looked like the whole old side of the plant was torn up. I didn't know it at the time, but my wife's first thought had been that our furnace that I had been cleaning and working on a few days before had blown up. I also didn't find out for a couple of days that our back storm door had also been damaged. It had been blown open by the blast and the metal frame warped and bent so bad that it wouldn't close, but the glass was not even scratched or cracked.

After explaining what I had seen to my wife I told her that I was going over to National Guard Headquarters at the Civic Auditorium. I was a squad leader in our National Guard unit at the time and from what I had seen while standing on the bridge I knew that Eastman and probably a lot of other folks were going to need a lot of help."

Chapter 8

Freddie Shepherd's account continues

When I got to the Civic Auditorium WO John Smith, and another fellow, whose name I can't remember, who were full time employees with the Guard, were getting in a jeep to go see what had happened. I got in the jeep with them and explained what I had heard and seen as we were driving over to Eastman, going in by Wilcox Drive.

As we were going by the warehouses that are near the road next to the Glass Plant, we saw a man who had a towel wrapped around him walking around in a daze between the warehouses and the road. We stopped and tried to help him as best we could through the fence. He was not physically hurt, but was plenty torn up mentally.

He had been in one of the shower houses when the explosion happened He didn't know where his clothes were or what had happened to the other people that had been in the showers with him. We convinced him to go back toward a gate so he could get some help and then we went on around the road and got as close as they would let us go.

John asked someone there if they needed the National Guard or other help. The man he was talking to said no. He was just doing his job and didn't know yet how bad the situation was, or that all their emergency equipment had been wrecked by the explosion and they would soon be accepting all the help they could get.

We went back to headquarters and John started making some calls, trying to find out what the Guard could or should do at this time.

He was told there was nothing we could do officially until someone at Eastman or in the city government asked for help.

If the situation was as bad as John had told them, the best thing we could do was start getting ready so that when the call did come we could move as fast as possible.

I went back home to put on my uniform and to take my wife to her mom and dad's on East Center Street. I didn't know how long I would be out with the Guard that night or if there might be more explosions and East Center Street is a whole lot farther away from Eastman than East Sevier is.

By the time I got back to Guard headquarters several more men had shown up and some of us took jeeps and drove around to see how much damage had been done to the downtown area.

As we drove down Center Street in the area of where Sevier crosses it, one store had the front plate glass window out and a man was sitting in a chair in the window with a shot gun across his lap. Every time we drove by there that night he was sitting there.

Several stores had broken windows, but we didn't notice any serious damage. By the time we got back several more men had shown up. We were divided up into teams of three or four each and told to patrol the downtown area and help out where ever we were needed.

I was riding around in a jeep with my platoon sergeant and sometime early in the evening he got word that a close friend of his who worked at Eastman was missing and we started checking in with the hospital every hour or so to try to get some news.

It was during one of these checks that someone at the hospital said that a tractor-trailer with medical supplies was on its way from Atlanta and they would appreciate us helping unload it when it got here. We said we would get more help and be back."

Chapter 9

Freddie Shepherd's account continues

Sometime around ten o'clock, I remembered that I was supposed to be at work that night and we drove back out to Eastman where I found one of the fellows that I worked with going in the gate and I told him to tell our foreman that I wouldn't be in that night.

While there we tried to find out what the situation was and found out there were still some fires out of control and a real danger of an even worse explosion if the fires got to a hydrogen plant.

Every once in a while there would be a small explosion and fireball when drums of chemicals in one of the burning buildings would explode. Ambulances and rescue vehicles were continuing to make their rounds from Eastman's medical building and the hospital. Some rescue folks were going directly from the blast site to the hospital.

When we got back to the hospital I saw a fellow that I had grown up with was driving one of the ambulances and working with some of the rescue folk.

He said it was a real nightmare out there, and that in one of the torn up buildings he had found a fellow we had gone to school with. There were tears in his eyes as he was telling me all of this. It was about that same time that we found out that my platoon sergeant's friend had also died in the initial blast.

I don't remember the exact time that the truck hauling the medical supplies arrived, but I'll never forget the face of the driver after he backed that truck up to the loading dock and was told what was going on. He said that he had been loading groceries to haul back to Oakwood when he got word to quit loading the groceries and get the rig over to a medical supply warehouse as soon as possible.

After the medical supplies were loaded he had a police escort out of Atlanta. At the city line he was met by the Georgia State Police who escorted him to the Tennessee line where he was met by the Tennessee Highway Patrol who brought him to the Kingsport City Limits where the city police escorted him the rest of the way.

He didn't know what was really going on until he got to the hospital. He had only been told that there had been a bad explosion in Kingsport, there was a critical need for the medicine and that he would have a police escort all the way. He said that was the fastest trip he had ever had coming from Atlanta, and hadn't stopped or slowed down for anything since leaving the medical supply warehouse.

A lot of the medical supplies he had brought were needed to treat the victims who had come into contact with the aniline and other chemicals. Boxes and crates of groceries were all mixed up with the medical supplies as a result of being bounced around by the fast trip.

We had to unload almost half the groceries in order to find all the medical supplies. One hospital official kept complaining about the groceries, saying he didn't see why they couldn't have put the medicine on a truck by its self. So much for gratitude.

Turns out that the truck had been offered when someone at Oakwood heard that the medicine was needed and remembered that they had a truck in Atlanta getting ready to bring groceries back.

After unloading the truck we took a coffee break in the hospital cafeteria then continued our patrols around town, getting back to the Civic Auditorium sometime after daylight on October 5.

So far as I know there were no problems of any kind, looting, etc. that night. All I can remember is everyone pitching in to help out.

Since Tuesday, October 4 would have been my last graveyard shift, I didn't have to go back into work until 3 to 11 on Friday, and, O yeah, Eastman did pay me a couple of months later for the shift of work I missed that night. I also picked up pieces of metal out of our yard every time I mowed the next summer."

Chapter 10

James Wilcox still has vivid recollections of the terrible event.

"I can remember this day in my mind just like it was yesterday," he said.

"I was just getting off from work at the Eastman and had just passed by the building heading for my car when the explosion happened.

"The ground shook so hard that it picked me up off the ground and shook me until I couldn't see. It held on to me for a few seconds, then let me go. At that moment I jumped under a big Buick car for protection.

"All around me I saw and heard glass breaking and steel falling. There was so much noise from all that was going on! It seemed I was under the car a long time, but it was really only about 3 minutes.

"When the commotion calmed down enough for me to come out, I saw all the mess that had happened. I could see so much blood and knew there were a lot of people hurt and killed.

"I lost some good friends that day...that day I will never be able to forget."

****

His wife has strong memories of the calamity as well: "I also remember that day so vividly that I can recall every detail of what I was doing," she said.

"I was in the kitchen fixing dinner for my family and husband James, who worked at the Eastman, when all of a sudden my dishes in the cabinets started shaking and there was such a loud noise that me and my children went out on the porch, and right then I knew that something had exploded at Eastman.

"I felt so scared, wondering and worrying about my husband that I was very weak from thinking of what could be wrong.

"I went in the house and turned on the radio to see what I could find out.

"My fears were confirmed that there had been an explosion at the Eastman. There was not a lot of details at this time, so my mind was running wild with fear. I could see a huge dark, black sky above me from all the smoke coming up from the building that had exploded.

"My four little children were scared and crying and I was pacing around my yard, wanting so bad to find out what all had happened, but so scared to really know.

After about an hour, I was still in my yard crying, when at last my husband was driving up the driveway.

"It was a very sad time and a lot of people we knew were hurt or killed in that awful accident. I am so thankful that my James was able to come home to me, but I knew not all were so fortunate as to see a loved one come home on that dreadful afternoon."

Chapter 11

Virgil Bellamy, electrician for Bays Mountain Construction Company, Eastman's construction arm, had stopped by the Aniline Plant just ten minutes or so before shift change. Usif Haney, operator at the Aniline Plant, was very much involved and interested in the Palmer Center for Crippled Children in Kingsport and had managed to pick up some surplus intercoms at TEC. He hoped that Bellamy would be able to install them at the Palmer Center.

"They would be a lot of help, Virgil," he said.

"I'll be glad to install them," Bellamy replied, "but tell me just exactly where you want them."

Haney explained in detail, and even sketched out a plan on a bit of scrap paper.

Neither of the men realized that this would be one of the last things he would do.

Minutes later, shortly after Bellamy pulled his car out of the parking lot, the first explosion went off.

"The whole plant seemed to shake," he recalled.

"I had already pulled out in to the street, and was up at the railroad bridge, so I went on home. But as soon as I got there, my wife said they had already called for me to come back to the plant. My uncle owned a restaurant near Gibbons Lumber, and I stopped there. My dad, who worked in the shop at Eastman, was there, his face bloody and cut up. I couldn't tell how badly he was hurt, so I decided to take him to a doctor. The hospital in Kingsport was too crowded, I knew, so I decided to take him over to Gate City to his regular doctor. But when we got over to Clouds Ford, I met my brother, who had heard about the explosion and was starting over there to see about dad and myself. I told him they were already calling for me to come back to do electrical work, and asked him to take Dad on to the doctor, which he did.

"I drove back to town, and started up Lincoln Street, but the police had the road blocked and wouldn't let me through. I told him they had called for me to come back to work, and he said I could go up to Konnarock Road and go in that way. I did, and they were waiting for me up there at the gate and took me in.

"I was down there almost all night. It was a mess, a real wreck. There were dead men here and there, and body parts scattered around.

"We worked as long as we could, trying to get power cut off some places and back on in others. Charlie Sipe, who was in charge of Bays Mountain came around and told us to go home, and get a little rest, and be ready for a long, full day coming up. That was long after midnight.

"But be back down here at daylight," he said. "We've got to get this mess straightened out."

"I didn't know until the next day that Usif Haney was one of the two men who were literally blown to bits by the blast. They never found either body, only parts and pieces."

Chapter 12

The story broke hour by hour, with more details and facts concerning the tragedy becoming available with each passing minute.

By morning, it was known that the number of deaths would certainly make the explosion the largest disaster in the plant's history, as well as the towns and areas.

Eleven bodies had been found, and by midnight, nine of them had been identified. It became apparent that more deaths had occurred, and speculations as to the total number that would finally be announced ranged to twenty-five or more.

The morning newspaper, on Oct. 5, 1960, printed several hours earlier than usual, was on the streets before midnight, a full three hours prior to its usual time.

The lead story, by executive editor **Ellis Binkley**, screamed across the black and white page with a headline as large as the one that proclaimed the end of World War II a few years previously.

"BLAST KILLS 11" it read. **"60 OTHERS HURT AT EASTMAN"**

There was a smaller headline below
"Whole City Feels Shock".

Bink's story told the grim facts:

"An earth-jarring explosion at Tennessee Eastman Company late yesterday afternoon left 11 known dead and more than 60 injured.

At midnight nine of the dead had been identified. Two others were unidentified. TEC listed the following dead: Bernard Arnold, 50, 249 Dee Lee Rd.; Manze Powers, 50, Jonesboro; John Squibb, 44, Telford, TN, Rural Route 4; E. O. Repass, 51, Hilton, Va., Rural Route 1; Jimmy W. Sanders, 27, Blountville, Rural Route 3; Andrew J. Chadwell, 29, South Holston Hills Rd.; Arthur H. Stevens, 44, Indian Springs, Rural Route 1; Cornelius Y. Depew, 36, Church Hill, Rural Route 3; Carl Cochran, 53, Fall Branch.

The blast occured at 4:45 p.m. in the aniline plant at TEC and was followed by a fire. The fire was brought under control at 8 o'clock and was declared "out" an hour later.

The plant where the accident occured is in the organic chemical division of the Eastman works.

Most of the injured suffered cuts from flying glass. Hundreds of panes of glass were blown from windows in all areas of the 400 acre plant.

47 Remain in Hospital

The injured were sent to the Holston Valley Community Hospital from the Eastman Medical Department. The company said 47 were admitted to the hospital.

Late last night officials said an estimate of the damage could not be made until daylight. They did say the immediate area of the explosion received extensive damage.

The building in which the blast occured was built 18 months ago.

Other parts of some operating areas were shut down in a controlled manner as a precautionary measure. Most of the balance of the plant will be back in operation by today, a company announcement said.

There are more than 160 buildings at Tennessee Eastman, which is Tennessee's largest industrial plant.

Chapter 13

Ellis Binkley's account continues:

Jars Whole City

This is the most serious accident ever to occur at the plant in its 40 year history. The second most serious was April 3, 1953, when four were killed and three injured in an explosion in the research laboratory.

The blast jarred downtown Kingsport and was felt as far away as Johnson City. Many homes in the residential area near the plant were damaged.

Offers of help came immediately from nearby towns. At one time there were 25 ambulances lined up ready to rush the injured to the hospital.

Several towns called to offer rescue squads, blood and other assistance. At least five rescue squads were on hand.

A line of blood donors formed at the hospital. Many were used to build up a reserve of blood for the more seriously injured.

The Salvation Army set up a mobile canteen and dispensed food and drink to the fire fighters and rescue workers.

Soon after the explosion, telephone switchboards at TEC, the Kingsport Times-News and other places were swamped with calls seeking information. For hours, only *emergency long-distance calls were accepted. The public relations office at TEC went on an emergency basis and was releasing information as fast as it became available.*

Rumors spread over the area like wild fire. They had the dead numbered in the scores and the injured in the hundreds.

TEC's public relations office released the names of the fatally injured only after they had been checked by the personnel office and the next of kin notified.

This caused some delay in releasing the names, but the list was as accurate as the company could make it.

Four telephone lines in the public relations office were kept busy with calls from news media from all over the country. Two of the calls were from London, England newspapers.

Here is a partial list of those hospitalized, as obtained from HVCH and TEC records:

Don Baldwin, 1605 LaSalle St.; Harry Bishop, 3905 Summit Drive; Lucian Blalock, Route 4, Hiltons, Va.; W. T. Bostic, 1222 Cherry St.; Clarence Byers, 258 Walker St.; J. D. Byington, Route 1, Church Hill.

Ezra Carter, Clinchport, Va.; Wesley Collings, Route 6, Kingsport; Carl Box, Route 7, Jonesboro; Mrs. Irene Crumley, Route 10, Kingsport; Elmer A. Ford, 1638 "C" Street, Kingsport; Ray E. Ford, Route 7, Jonesboro.

J. W. Gott, Hiltons, Va.; M. T. Herron, Route 1, Gate City, Va.; Charles Hughes, Surgoinsville; S. D. Johnson, Box 123, Gate City; Corbin Lane, 236 Virginia St.; G. W. Mellon, 115 East Carters Valley Road; Charles Minton, Box 95, Gate City; U. W. Munsey, Route 11, Kingsport; Sandford Neeley, 1429 Dobyns Drive; Mrs. Doris Orfield, 3202 Ridgeview Dr.; Dr. Paul J. Parker, Route 4, Church Hill; Roy Rachel, Route 3, Kingsport.

W. S. Shaw, 1505 Waverly Road; Virgil Smith, Route 2, Surgoinsville; Mike Sovic, 1116 Lowell Drive; W. R. Stallard, Route 6, Kingsport; Claud Story, 2609 Heatherly Lane and Ralph Waters, 726 Riverside Avenue.

These names were reported by the hospital, but addresses were unavailable:

Conner Caldwell, Henry Carter, William C. Evans, W. G. Head and Lee Murray."

Chapter 14

Frank Creasy, City Editor of the Times, had rushed to the scene as well. His story took a more human interest slant, from a rescue workers view.

"Please God, Let It Rain Hard," the heading read.
"At 7:45 last night a few drops of rain fell on stone-faced, feverish fire fighters and rescue workers around the Tennessee Eastman Company holocaust.

"Please God. . .Let it rain. . .Let it rain hard," said one of the volunteers as he looked skyward from the grip of a stretcher. The man on the stretcher was dead.

Small explosions compared to the mushrooming first blast - were still batting flames and debris over the area. The workers and tense onlookers had been warned repeatedly of the possibility of another explosion which might even be more devastating than the original.

The single prayer was "God, help us bring this under control." Forty-five minutes later the word was passed that "the fire seems to be contained". Weary crews turned their thoughts to the task of searching the area for the bodies. There was no way of knowing last night exactly how many were injured.

TEC's medical department, Holston Valley Community Hospital and Munal Clinic took care of them as fast as possible.

This reporter counted 41 walking casualties while standing in one place at HVCH two hours later after the explosion. Many had already been released. We interviewed more than 20 persons who said they were within 100 to 300 feet of the first earth shaking explosion. Nobody was able to say exactly where the blast occured or its cause.

Doyle McLain said he was working atop a railroad car no more than 100 feet from the blast.

"I couldn't say I heard it or saw it" McLain said. "All I know was all of a sudden I didn't know where I was. It didn't knock me out though, I don't think. . .bricks were falling all around me. . .I put my hands over my head."

McLain said several more men were working close to him. He didn't know what happened to them. He received a number of minor cuts, and one nasty gash on his forehead. "I must be the luckiest man alive," he said.

C. W. Moseley, K. E. Depew, J. D. Williams and Jim Templeton all had similar statements. They were in or around the organic chemical buildings.

"I was in the machine shop. It knocked me down, and something fell on my leg," Moseley said. "As soon as I could get up I ran outside. The building (the aniline plant) was gone, and everything was on fire."

All of the men said they "had no idea" what touched off the explosion. Bill Hawkins, an inactive member of the Kingsport Lifesaving Crew, was among the first volunteer workers to reach the scene. He and the crew he was with made repeated trips to within a few yards of the inferno.

"When I first got there, there were three or four men lying outside. I went to one, and he said, "Don't bother about me, I'm ok". He got up and tried to help one of the others," Hawkins said.

"Everybody in the area was bleeding...it literally rained debris...glass, bricks, and metal for several minutes," Hawkins continued. *"We didn't even try to help anybody who was able to walk."* Hawkins estimated he was at the scene *"three or four minutes after the explosion".* Hawkins also said after three hours of work, *"You can't even tell where a building was down there. It looks like a great big garbage dump."*

Chapter 15

Frank Creasy's account continues.

"Other lifesaving crewmen to arrive almost immediately were Sam Zimmerman, Jim Bacon, Wright Johnson and Walter Salyer. The complete local crew was there within minutes, as were police, highway patrolmen, firemen, and a score of ambulances.

Within the matter of an hour Life Saving Crews and ambulances from as far away as Pennington Gap, Va., Abingdon, Va., and Rogersville were working alongside the locals. A crew even came from Knoxville.

Gate City, Johnson City, Bristol and other close-by towns sent off-duty policemen. The neighboring officers helped to keep traffic moving on area highways. National Guard and Civil Defense Crews also took an active part in rescue work. Salvation Army, Red Cross and other volunteer agencies quickly brought in their facilities.

As the first ambulances of injured arrived at HVCH the call went out for blood donors. Less than an hour later more volunteers than could be handled were standing in line to give blood. The force of the blast - which sent a black cloud mushrooming into the sky at 4:45 broke thousands of windows in homes and businesses within a 3-mile radius. Many of the injured were in office buildings hundreds of yards away at TEC.

Phil Coates was one of the workers at the TEC Research Building, approximately a quarter of a mile away.

"It shook the entire building like it was right under us," Coates said, "I actually thought it was our building."

A piece of metal weighing perhaps 25 pounds knocked a hole in the front of the house of Frank Jones, 2 Edgewood Village - which is about 500 yards away.

A piece of metal zoomed through the windshield and out the opposite side of an auto traveling toward the city on Lincoln St. City Police Cpl. Albert Fletcher said he did not know who the auto belonged to, or if anybody was hurt.

Cpl. Fletcher was at Police Headquarters when he heard the blast. "I got there as fast as I could," he said. "The first of the injured I saw were two men running from the fire. They were bloody all over, and didn't have on a stitch of clothes."

"A passing car stopped and took them to the hospital," he said.

The estimated property damage will also include many automobiles parked in lots near the blast. Virtually every car within 100 yards was damaged and there were perhaps 10 total losses.

One of the rescue workers found a visitors pass and a pair of dress shoes in the blast area. They were unexplained. Miraculously, nobody was reported seriously hurt at the adjoining Blue Ridge Glass Corp. Two or three were reported treated for cuts from flying glass. John D. Robbins and Elmer Jones said they were working in the Blue Ridge building closest to TEC. They said the entire side of the building fell under the force.

"I was hauling a load of glass on the electric truck," Robbins said. "It knocked me off, but didn't knock me out. The smoke and dust were so thick you couldn't see your hand in front of your face." Jones shook his head and said,

"If we've got a piece of glass which isn't broken, I don't know where it is".

Blue Ridge guard Sam Haney said the concussion "lifted me two feet off the ground." Haney showed a piece of jagged metal 8 inches across which he said landed a few feet from him. Other reports of "shrapnel" came in from numerous sources."

Chapter 16

We got word from the Tennessee State Highway Patrol about 11 pm that night that it had been alerted to give assistance to a truck loaded with a special drug shipment for a hospital in Kingsport, where an explosion and fire had killed at least 11 persons and injured 60 others. Local police units were dispatched to points along the route the truck was scheduled to take, alerted to be of any possible assistance. Because there was, at that time, only one hospital in Kingsport, we knew that Holston Valley Community Hospital was the destination.

Local police units said the truck had left Atlanta about 9:30 pm and would arrive in Kingsport sometime in the very early hours the following day. I began to hear other horror stories about the blast early that day. As an advertising representative of the newspaper, I had a regular schedule of clients to call on, ranging from downtown Kingsport to Gate City, Virginia.

In order to serve those firms, I had worked out a schedule of calls, assigning certain weekdays to different areas around town. Grocery ads were prime accounts, and both Tuesday and Thursday afternoons were regular call days for the three major food firms in town.

On Wednesday, I called on firms in Lynn Garden, Morrison City, Weber City, and Gate City, taking those on the right side of the road going over and those on the opposite side on the way back.

On that Wednesday morning, just hours after the blast, I took a few copies of the latest paper off the press along with me, in case they might be asked for. A newspaper advertising representative does more than just call on clients for advertising. Much more.

He or she is the representative of the newspaper to business firms, and, insofar as those firms are concerned, he or she is the newspaper. A good rep will write the news stories about the business firms called on, when they receive awards or honors, have new employees, or otherwise accomplish something that is note worthy. The rep will make pictures, sell newspapers, take subscriptions, collect bills, deliver invoices and tear sheets, talk to factory and distributor people about increased co-op allowances, make advertising layouts, plan schedules and campaigns, create art work and logos, and do a multitude of other odds and ends not normally associated with the business of simply soliciting advertising. I had a file of ideas, gleaned from a large number of out-of-town newspapers that might be useful to my accounts. When I noticed a clever ad in one of the out-of-state newspapers that came to the newsroom, I would clip it and file it away, a ready idea that could be available when needed or when the occasion presented itself.

The advertising services most newspapers buy are a good source for ideas and artwork as well, and I would try to think up different slants and sales ideas for various firms using the material available from them. Nothing pleases a newspaper ad man more than seeing one of his accounts succeed, and I was fortunate enough to see a good many success stories.

On the other side of the coin, there are always a few failures; hopefuls that sink investment money into a business and simply cannot make a go of it, no matter how hard they seem to try. Business failures of this kind hurts everyone involved; the firm itself and its owners; the creditors, the employees, the general business community, and the newspaper, who loses the potential of a good regular advertiser for further future income. There is an ethic, ignored by some and unknown by others, that should control the sales efforts of an advertising representative.

Chapter 17

In those days, an ad rep was a confidant, business advisor, and public relations counselor to the accounts on his or her list.

Some ad reps try to squeeze every dollar possible out of the account, hoping to be considered heroes by their boss or the newspaper publisher.

There is also the ad rep who simply picks up pre-planned or set advertising from chain stores and large firms that have their own advertising departments; a job that can be handled by almost anyone with a good smile and reasonably good manners.

But like any other sort of job, you get from it just what you put in to it. Because I hoped to one day run a newspaper of my own, large or small, I made an effort to try and give my accounts the kind of assistance and service they needed to help build their success.

From Jack Huffaker, the grand old man in the advertising department, I had learned the value of drinking coffee with clients.

Jack had started his selling career as a ragamuffin newsboy on the streets of downtown Knoxville, before the turn of the century. He graduated to department store clerking by age twelve, and got his first pair of long pants along with that job.

As a young man, Jack became a "traveling drummer," riding the train from town to town, stopping at a likely place, renting a buggy and driver to haul him and his sample case out on his quest for sales.

In larger towns, he would rent a hotel room and invite businessmen to come there to see his wares.

At last, weary of the road and constant travel, Jack took a job as manager of a store in Johnson City. The firm was owned by a Knoxville concern, and his daily reports were made directly to the owner.

One day, a telegram came to the Johnson City store, instructing Jack to go do a bit of investigating.

"They said there was a town starting up, called Kingsport, about twenty five or thirty miles from Johnson City," he told me once. "They told me to go over there and see if it would be a good place to start another store."

Jack caught the train and made the trip the very next day. "It was a mess," he said. "There was one street, where the Depot was, and a big, wide mud hole where they were trying to grade out a wide place with mules and drag pans (which later became Broad Street) and about two or three little store buildings. It sure looked dismal."

"I got back on the train and went back to Johnson City," Jack said. "I sent a telegram to my boss and told him that if the world ever had a rear end, it was Kingsport, and that there was no possibility whatever that a store could make it there."

"A couple of years later," he said, with a rueful grin, "I was over there trying to rent any kind of space I could to put in my own store. The town had grown almost overnight and it was booming. I guess the birth of Kingsport as a city was the most exciting time for business that I can ever recall."

How he got into the newspaper business is another story, and must be passed by for now. But he knew more about business and retail and public relations than any man I've ever known.

"If you want to sell advertising in this town," he told me the first day I worked for him, "make friends. Because it is a whole lot easier to sell your friends than it is to sell people who don't know you and maybe don't like your looks."

Sound advice that could well be applied today.

Chapter 18

The first story about the explosion I heard was from one of the local firemen who happened to be having breakfast at the Smoke House, Bob Harkleroad's little restaurant on Market Street.

I had stopped in for a quick cup of coffee before driving out to Lynn Garden and making my usual calls from there to Gate City and back.

The fireman looked up and waved me over to his table when I walked in. "You go out there to the Eastman yesterday, to cover that?" he asked.

When you work for a newspaper, most folks think you do most everything, write stories, make photos, set type and sell ads. That is sometimes true, on smaller newspapers, especially weeklies, but not usually the case.

"No," I replied. "I drove out that way and ran up the sidewalk to the Glass Plant just after the blast went off, but when I found out what had happened, I went back to the newspaper. Were you up there?"

"I was there almost all night," he said. "It was horrible. We kept finding bits and pieces of people." He told about finding arms and legs that had been blown off by the tremendous explosion. From his stories and other tales I picked up that day, I pieced together the following accounts:

Firemen Cecil Rose, Horton King, and Gilbert Parker were on the first fire truck to arrive at the plant site.

Their truck, stationed at Fire Station No. 2 on Memorial Boulevard, beside the Civic Auditorium, was in charge of Captain C. B. Kilgore.

These firemen recalled three distinct, loud, horrible explosions, all coming near together. Parker was under his car, working on it at the time the first blast went off. He had taken a creeper out of the Station house to use in examining the muffler or tailpipe on his vehicle, which needed to be repaired, and had just rolled under the car to take a look when he heard the first explosion. He immediately rolled out from under the car and jumped to his feet as he heard a second loud boom go off, drawing his attention toward the sound. He saw, he later said, the top of a brick building rising above the tree line, just like a launched rocket! Two men, or what appeared to be two men, were on the roof of the building as it rose up in the air.

The structure seemed to stall in mid air, and the lower portion of it began to disintegrate, with bricks falling away as it collapsed from bottom to top and fell away.

The third loud explosion went off as the sight dropped from view. The fireman thought the explosion must have been at the Blue Ridge Glass Plant, or at Cal Gas, the bottled gas plant nearby.

King, Rose and Parker raced to their fire truck and jumped in, taking their assigned positions automatically as the big red machine roared out of the station and raced toward the scene. King was on truck duty, Parker at tailboard.

They raced toward what they thought was the site of the explosion, and discovered it to be the Eastman plant, rather than the Glass or Gas firms.

The first scene to meet their eyes was the body of a man, smashed against the steel gatepost at the railroad gate, his body pressed partly into the post. To the left, chemical tanks were steaming, and burst pipes were sticking up and out the ground all around, "thick as a cane break" it was later said.

A woman, dressed in skirt, blouse, and high heels came running out of a building to the left, behind some tanks, raced between them, running on thin, tall spike heels. She ran toward the high chain link fence, which towered above her from its ten foot height, went right up the fence, climbed half way up, put her foot to the barbwire strands at the top of the fence, and over she went, to land in the street outside, feet first, where her shoes stuck up in the pavement, the high heels buried in the melting asphalt. She ran right out of the shoes and kept going, not missing a step!

Broken steam pipes were everywhere, barrels of chemicals were constantly exploding, men were running in screaming mobs toward the gates shrieking and yelling at the tops of their voices. Two men came running out, among the falling brick.

Chapter 19

A steel lintel from a destroyed building came flying through the air with a "whusk, whusk, wusk, sound, spinning around like the propeller on the top of a helicopter or a lawn mower blade. "Good God!" one of the men yelled. "Look! There's some man's leg!" Momentum carried him another twenty feet. "My God!" he cried. "It's MY leg!" He had been running, how cannot be explained, on one leg. The flying lintel had struck his leg and cut it off, with him still moving. The lintel crashed through the gateway, went across the street and slammed into a new Buick automobile that was parked there. It cut the door and front seats off, went all the way through and embedded itself in the car parked in the space beyond it.

Safety plugs in steam pipes had ruptured all around the plant, and steam filled the air with both sight and sound, the escaping hiss of steam making a terrifying racket. A huge natural gas line going to one of the buildings had broken, topped up, pointing into the air, and flames were shooting out of its end like a giant blow torch.

All the flames and explosions had caused a fire storm, resulting in what fireman call a "cool fire." The strength of the flames drew cardboard boxes and debris into itself. Firemen were able to work close to the blaze, because the flames were drawing back into themselves.

Chemical tanks, containing unknown materials, were a great worry. Barrels kept exploding, sending pieces of steel flying through the air like bullets from an attacking enemy invasion force.

One of the firemen later reported that as he worked near a loading dock, he was able to fasten his hose to a steel beam and kept it aimed at the flames while he often ducked under the concrete dock to avoid being hit by the flying bits of steel. A steel beam smashed down, landing within inches of his position. A part of a man's jaw and an ear were hanging on the collapsed beam.

There were reports that the most gruesome discovery was made behind one of the devastated buildings. A human brain, intact as though it had been removed by a talented surgeon, lay on a cross tie on the railroad track just as if it had been carefully placed there. These stories never got into print, of course, being considered too gruesome for a family newspaper that might be read by some of the victim's survivors.

Those who recall the tragic explosion will remember the details of where they were and what they were doing all of their lives.

Mollie Lynch Click, and her husband, James Ed Click, now deceased, were visiting friends on Redwood Drive that day.

"We were standing in the back door looking down toward TEC when we heard the explosion and saw a mushroom cloud rise with the body of a person a little above the cloud, then the cloud enveloped the person while the body was still ascending. There was a round cast iron cover or lid, similar to a manhole cover, which landed in the back yard as we watched.

"A TEC employee was sent to pick up debris and made arrangements to do repairs."

Chapter 20

Margaret Ball, of Fall Branch, had brought her children, Kenny and Elizabeth, to meet her husband Glen, at Gate #8. Glen had worked the day shift in the Color Lab at the Tenite Department. The lab workday was over, and all the workers had gone for the day. The Ball family headed for Pal's Drive In, in downtown Kingsport, for a hotdog supper, a special treat for the children, for that was their favorite place to eat. The family planned to go to the grocery store after eating.

As their car rolled along New Street, just a block from the restaurant, they suddenly heard a terrific explosion.

"We were almost in front of Olan Mills Studio when we heard it," Margaret said, "our car seemed to rise all the way up off the ground! It was almost like a bomb had exploded nearby.

"The glass windows fell out of all the buildings; there was broken glass everywhere.

"We drove over to Main Street and out to Sullivan, on to the underpass. Glen decided at this time to return home and get the camera. Then we drove back to McKinney Street in Springdale, and made pictures from the top of the ridge there, as the explosions continued for some time.

"My uncle, John Grills, lived on McKinney. He was injured in the explosion, but recovered from his injuries and returned to work."

* * * * *

"I normally worked the 8 to 5 shift in the AY Division, but I was off on that Oct. 4th," **Harrison L. (Red) Taylor** said. "I had been mowing the yard and stopped to get a drink and to speak with my wife. When I came back outside the mower wouldn't start. I had just removed the spark plug when the mower started to buck and jump. I though it was going to blow up on me, when I noticed that the ground and the house were shaking too. My pull up style garage door slammed shut, that was when I heard two explosions that sounded like bombs going off. "I could see black smoke in the sky to the southeast and I knew something was wrong. I ran into the house to check on my wife and see if anything was damaged. The shaking had been so violent I couldn't believe there wasn't anything broken. I had my wife turn on the radio to see if we could find out what had happened.

"There was such confusion, it was a little while before they finally confirmed it was the Eastman that had exploded. Within an hour it was announced over the radio that blood was desperately needed. If you could give, go straight to the hospital. I left right then for the hospital. There were 3 lines and a doctor and nurse were going down the lines asking if you knew your blood type. If you did, you had to get in the line coming from the emergency room. At one time the line came from the ER (it was on the same side as the old nurses building at that time), all the way across the front of the hospital down to Ravine Street. I saw nurses from the Eastman and doctor's offices, that I knew helping with all the ones that had been hurt and those of us giving blood. It seemed like everyone had come out to help. "I stood in line for about 3 hours, and I was next in line through the door when a doctor came out and said they had enough blood for the time being, but, they would call if they needed more.

"My brother Frank was working in the AY that day and we had to wait to find out if he was o.k. He finally managed to get word home that he was alright about 7 o'clock that night. Later that night we sat on our front porch and watched balls of fire going straight up in the sky from barrels exploding.

"I lived on Stone Drive then, about 6 miles from the Eastman. Being able to feel, hear and see the explosions from there, I knew it had to be bad. I knew some of those that were killed and when I returned to work and and saw the devastation the explosion had caused, I knew the memory of that day would always be with me."

Chapter 21

When the afternoon newspaper came out, some of the stories had been updated slightly, but it was much the same, a repeat of the morning edition that had been re-hashed.

Ellis Binkley's story again had the lead, but the headline and the first few paragraphs had been changed.

BLAST TOLL 13
Eleven Identified;
Two Lost,
Presumed Dead

"The death toll as the result of a terrific explosion at Tennessee Eastman Company late yesterday afternoon now stands at 13. More than 60 were injured in the blast.

Of the known dead 11 have been identified. Two are missing and are presumed dead, a company official said this morning.

The company listed the following dead: James W. Sage, Jr., 28, Indian Springs; J. D. Mullins, 39, 401 Chadwell Rd.; Bernard Arnold, 50, 249 Dee Lee Rd.; Manze Powers, 50, Jonesboro; John Squibb, 44, Telford, Tenn.; E. O. Repass, 51, Hiltons, Va.; Jimmie W. Sanders, 27, Blountville; Dr. Andrew J. Chadwell, 29, South HolstonHills Rd.; Arthur H. Stevens, 44, Indian Springs,; Cornelius Y. Depew, 36, Church Hill; Carl Cochran, 53, Fall Branch.

Missing and presumed dead: Usif Haney, 45, Preston Woods; Jess Ray Shell, 36, 431 Wilma St.

James C. White, TEC president, said this morning:

"This is the worst disaster Tennessee Eastman Company has suffered in its 40 years of operation. Our deepest sympathy goes to the families of those lost and injured. The company wishes to thank everyone in Kingsport, and the surrounding area, who so effectively mobilized to aid us at this tragic time."

The blast occurred at 4:45 p.m. in the aniline plant at TEC and was followed by a fire. The fire was brought under control at 8 o'clock and was declared "out" an hour later.

The plant where the accident occurred is in the organic chemicals division of the Eastman works.

Most of the injured suffered cuts from flying glass. Hundreds of panes of glass were blown from windows in all areas of the 400 acre plant.

47 Remain in Hospital

The injured were sent to the Holston Valley Community Hospital from the Eastman Medical Department. The company said 47 were admitted to the hospital.

This morning 39 were still in the hospital. In addition to those in HVCH, at least eight are in other hospitals and clinics in the area, it was announced.

A company official said no attempt was made to keep a record of those treated for superficial wounds and released.

"We were more interested in treating, than in counting the people yesterday afternoon," he said. However he did say that the total injured is more than 60.

Company officials said today that facilities in the immediate area of the explosion received extensive damage. An accurate estimate cannot be made until later.

Hospital Admissions Cut Down

Dr. H. Jim Brown, president of the Holston Valley Community Hospital medical staff and William A. Phillips, executive director of the hospital, this morning released the following statement:

"There will be no elective medical or surgical admissions to the hospital until the effect of the emergency admissions following the Tennessee Eastman explosion can be fully determined."

Some Injured
Treated at JC

At least three persons were treated at Memorial Hospital in Johnson City. They were: John Looney, 18, Johnson City, admitted with broken shoulder; Allie Bowser, 45, Rt. 11, dismissed; Howard Conner, Rt. 11, admitted with leg injury.

Looney said: "I was about 14 feet away when the plant blew up. It knocked me down. I got up and started running and passed a man with a leg cut off. I saw another man lying on the ground. I guess he was dead."

Earle Henley of Johnson City, an insurance adjuster who was near the scene said: "it was like a giant hand reaching out; plate glass windows fell like rain."

Chemical trucks from the Olin-Mathieson Chemical Company in Saltville, Va., were rushed to Kingsport for the purpose of removing chemicals from the disaster area.

Chapter 22

Bill Barnett, a long time writer at the Times, just happened to be on hand at the hospital and observed the frenzy of activity first hand. Doing the natural thing for a newspaperman to do, Bill wrote his impressions and they were quickly made into a sidebar feature story.

Hospital Staff Proves Mettle in Swift, Efficient Action

(Staff member Bill Barnett was a patient at Holston Valley Community Hospital when the biggest explosion in Kingsport's history put the whole city in turmoil.)

"Holston Valley Hospital proved Tuesday night that it is ready for any emergency.

With so many emergency patients descending on a hospital at once you might expect chaos. Instead doctors, nurses, orderlies, volunteer helpers, all worked with swift efficiency that kept ahead of the need.

Even cooks and a few of the more able-bodied patients pitched in to help make up beds and otherwise prepare.

I was in my bed eating supper when a shock wave from the explosion more than two miles away shook the building. My roommate, who couldn't eat anyway because of an operation coming up the next day, went to investigate and reported the column of black smoke that was visible for miles.

We went to the room across the hall where the smoke could be seen. Mrs. Richard Gray, the patient in that room, commented she hoped the explosion wasn't at Eastman. Her husband would just be getting off work about then, she said.

Someone said he had just heard it was a glass plant. Mrs. Gray was reassured momentarily.

About then a call came over the public address system: "All doctors in the hospital please report to the emergency room."

Another call went out to all doctors and nurses in the city. They came in private cars and taxicabs at the same time the ambulances were bringing in the injured.

Every stretcher and wheelchair in the building was taken to the ground floor emergency room. Most of the nurses left their regular stations to help in the emergency room until off-duty nurses had time to get there. It worked so smoothly that I don't think a single regular patient was neglected.

A call was made for blood donors. Most of the office personnel in the front of the building headed back to the bloodbank room. About five minutes later hundreds of people from all over town began streaming-in in answer to a radio appeal for blood.

By then Mrs. Gray knew that the explosion had been at Eastman. Seeing a man she knew among the blood donors approaching the building, she called to him and asked him to check on her husband.

A crowd of other relatives of Eastman workers gathered outside the emergency entrance to see if they could recognize any of the injured being brought in.

When it began to appear that the stretchers and wheelchairs downstairs might not hold all the injured, practical nurses and volunteer helpers who had been making up beds to receive those admitted, started wheeling the beds down the halls, into elevators and then to the receiving area.

The roller-mounted beds made excellent stretchers, and the patients didn't have to be transferred to a bed when they came upstairs.

The hospital was fortunate in having a whole vacant wing and plenty of extra beds and bed clothes available for such an emergency as a result of the expansion two years ago.

It was thought at first that would be plenty of space without disturbing any of the patients already in the hospital. When I volunteered to check out a day early, I was told it wouldn't be necessary.

The man Mrs. Gray had asked to check on her husband reported Mr. Gray had been hurt slightly, but not enough to require admission to the hospital. He had been released after emergency treatment.

Mrs. Gray was still upset. "He would have told him to tell me he wasn't hurt badly even if he was."

I went to see if I could find out anything about Mr. Gray. I found those who were caring for the injured didn't know their names and didn't have time to find out. That could wait until later.

When I got back to my section of the hospital the situation had changed. It wasn't certain whether the formerly empty wing could hold all the injured after all. Those of us who had planned to check out the next day were asked to do so at once if possible. I went to my room to dress. Before leaving I asked about Mrs. Gray. She had received permission to go down to the emergency room to see if she could find her husband.

Her husband meanwhile had left the emergency room after treatment for his minor injury, waited patiently for *the visiting hour to begin at 7 pm and was standing in her doorway with the visitor's card in his hand waiting for her to come back from looking for him.*

I had to leave before the Gray's got together. It must have been a moving scene. It was the fastest I've ever known anyone to be discharged from a hospital. The front office just said we'd settle all the details later. But there was a transportation problem. I was told there was no use to call my wife to come after me, she couldn't get through the traffic. Only emergency vehicles and taxi cabs were allowed through.

After waiting for a cab, I sat next to a woman who had just had surgery that day. She, too, was leaving to make room for one of the injured. The cab driver couldn't get to the address I gave him, only three blocks away. Police waved him in the opposite direction, so I gave him the office address and had my wife pick me up there later."

Chapter 23

Barnett's story was enhanced, perhaps, by a companion piece by C. M. Chandler, another newsman. While Barnett told his story from a personal note, Chandler took a more detached, impersonal view. Both stories helped readers realize the magnitude of the tragic disaster.

Hospital Resembles Mine Disaster Scene

The outdoor public address system hypnotized hundreds - the grief stricken, the blood donors and the curious.

The scene at Kingsport's Holston Valley Community Hospital was reminiscent of the pictures of mine explosions - the same anxious faces watching ambulances, cars, and trucks arrive with the injured.

Highway patrolmen and volunteer workers separated the blood donors, the injured, other volunteer workers from the curious and the worried.

The public address system gave the names of those who had been injured, treated, assigned beds, or released. Sighs of relief could be heard after each group of names was read.

A few times there were cries of grief. One family was singing "Rock of Ages" as they were led away by sympathetic friends.

The hospital's hastily organized blood bank operated efficiently but couldn't keep up with the growing number of donors.

Hospital workers said "several hundred" persons answered the call for blood donations. Critically needed were types "O-positive" and "A-negative". There was no way of estimating the exact number of persons who gave blood.

Blood also was rushed to Kingsport from the blood banks of neighboring cities.

Donors filed through until 8:30 pm when the hospital staff requested all who weren't the immediate family of the victims to return to their homes and phone in their names and blood types.

Fifty to 60 members of the Ladies Auxiliary and the Junior Auxiliary provided assistance in uniting families with the injured. They offered what other aid and comfort they could.

Many hospital patients well enough to be moved, gave their beds and room to the explosion victims.

Volunteers assisted in directing traffic-channeling vehicles with the injured to the hospital. Others served coffee and sandwiches, and filled out nametags for the emergency cases and blood donors. Still others manned the entrances at the hospital-offering information and keeping order.

Transportation was urgently needed to remove the patients who had given up their beds. A plea was made on the public address system and again the people of Kingsport came through and provided the necessary automobiles. Some cases were driven to Greeneville, Erwin and points in Southwest Virginia.

Clergymen from the area were on hand to offer comfort.

Chapter 24

Tennessee's Governor Buford Ellington had been informed of the explosion almost immediately after it happened. He was quickly in contact with authorities and plant officials to assure them that the state government would do all possible to be of help. A lengthy telephone call was condensed into a few short paragraphs in the news item:

Ellington Offers Aid

Governor Buford Ellington was in touch with Kingsport authorities a short time after the tragic explosion at Tennessee Eastman Co.

The governor offered services of the National Guard if they were needed.

State Safety Commissioner Greg O'Rear was in touch with Kingsport Highway Patrol station and ordered all patrolmen in the area to take assignments from the local post headquarters.

Half the town, it seemed, was in shock. Those who were involved in the plant's work or had relatives or friends there, were anxious and fearful, for in some cases, word of injuries and damages was slow to be received. And, shattered plate glass windows in many places of business had made clerks and others nervous and jumpy. There was a story about that as well.

Store Windows are Shattered

In downtown stores Tuesday afternoon, employees and customers stood in shocked disbelief when plate glass windows shattered onto streets and sidewalks.

In most instances, passersby and employees of neighboring stores converged on each scene thinking perhaps the blast occurred within.

Business establishments with damage included Huddle Electric, Harrison's Bootery, Figurama Beauty Bar, Kingsport Federal, C&R Green Stamp, Broadstreet Furniture, Kingsport Times-News, Kingsport Automotive, Bill Stewart's Produce, Copeland Office Equipment.

Later in the night, a band of students and Boy Scouts patroled the streets with brooms and shovels cleaning up debris and glass. The Kingsport Utilities reported two power lines damaged. The major power trouble was on a 12,000 volt line which feeds Sullivan Gardens, Horse Creek Road section and Long Island.

A transmission circuit was out in the Borden Mills section. A spokesman for Utilities said repairmen were standing by to repair all damages reported into the office.

The A Company of the 370th Engineers, Army Reserve was called out to guard stores where windows were broken.

David McBride, another newspaper writer, told of his personal reaction on visiting the scene.

Faces Mirror
Horror, Fear

A mask of frozen horror contorted faces when I reached the scene of a devastating explosion at Tennessee Eastman Company here Tuesday afternoon.

Debris was still falling when I drove into the area amidst a caravan of ambulances, rescue squads and curious onlookers.

Those already in the area were stunned by the bone-shattering blast and stood looking at the flaming holocaust in disbelief.

Inching as near into the shattering buildings as the intense heat would allow, I could see neither signs of life nor death.

Huge columns of smoke and fire belched skyward from the twisted ruins and escaping steam created a weird deafening scream.

Within minutes after the initial blast, firemen from Kingsport and several surrounding cities poured into the area but were forced back by the constant threat of more explosions.

Retreating to the evacuation quarters I watched as the injured were rushed to waiting ambulances. The horrified expressions of could-be relatives were moving.

One unidentified little boy stood viewing the tragic scene with tears streaming down his cheeks. "I think my daddy was in there," he cried. He could have been.

Other apparent relatives tried to gain entrance to the area but were turned back by the heavy guard force.

Another woman, who appeared to be in a state of shock, kept mumbling over and over, "He would have been off from work in a few minutes."

After stepping a few feet away to talk to another man I again turned in the direction of the woman, only to see her affectionately hugging a dirt-smeared man. She had found her husband and the two walked slowly away.

Darkness settled over the scene a little earlier than normal due to the heavy screen of black smoke hovering overhead.

At intervals, a huge ball of flame would erupt from the devastation and light the sky. As it did, the hundreds of onlookers would instinctively shift back for fear of another explosion.

Chapter 25

My own observation during those scant moments following the blast, when I had raced a-foot toward the bottled gas company I had thought to be the site of the blast, had shown me that Blue Ridge Glass Company had probably suffered considerable damage in those parts of the plant nearest the Eastman property. A news story confirmed that fact.

Blast Damages Blue Ridge Glass

Yesterday's blast in the Tennessee Eastman Chemical Building did extensive damage to the plant of The Blue Ridge Glass Division of America - St. Gobain Corp.

J. H. Lewis, Blue Ridge general manager, said that a preliminary survey indicated that damage to Blue Ridge buildings and equipment would amount to "several hundred thousand dollars."

Two Blue Ridge workmen suffered minor injuries from flying glass. The names of the two were not available.

The Special Products division of the Blue Ridge plant had the greatest damage. Lewis said that windows and doors in most of the Blue Ridge buildings were shattered and twisted and that there was extensive damage to walls and equipment in the Special Products Division.

He added that the company's furnaces and glass production facilities apparently escaped damage except for broken windows, doors, etc.

Work was halted in the Blue Ridge plant immediately after the blast, but cleanup operations got underway as soon as danger from the chemical fire abated and glass production was scheduled to resume this morning, Lewis said.

The Blue Ridge plant is situated some 300 yards away from the Eastman building which was wrecked by the blast.

There were a couple more news stories, one by Herb Parris and the other by Jerry Alley, both well known local newspapermen and fine writers. Herb had hurried to the scene from downtown, and, although it was his day off, pitched in and wrote his thoughts and reactions. Jerry had made a quick tour of the explosion site and the neighboring business area the morning after the disaster and reported on damages to buildings and homes.

As Smoke
Mushroomed,
Many Thought City Had Been Bombed

This reporter was in town yesterday buying paint for do-it-yourself chores at home, when, shortly before 5 pm, I stepped from a downtown store on Center Street and headed for my car and home.

Suddenly the buildings rocked on their foundations and a giant explosion split the air.

Across the street from me at Harrison's Bootery a pane of plate glass crashed to the sidewalk. A woman screamed and lunged into the street to escape, almost colliding with a passing auto.

Over the Kingsport National Bank a giant pillar of smoke mushroomed into the sky.

My first thoughts, as were the thoughts of many others I learned later, were that some alien country had bombed Tennessee Eastman Company.

Could scenes of war which I had witnessed only a few years ago have come to this country?

A few minutes later I was at the scene of the explosion.

Chapter 26

Newspaper accounts of the tragedy continue:

The Medical Center at Eastman was overflowing with the injured receiving emergency treatment and awaiting the arrival of ambulances.

Strangers became friends. The injured aided the injured. A man, limping and with one arm in a sling, comforted a fellow workman who had suffered a head injury. Everywhere, paid and volunteer workmen scurried to lend their aid. At the scene of the explosion, ambulances and rescue workers moved in to pick up the injured. Firemen trained hoses on the flame that billowed from various plant buildings.

Would there be other explosions?

Despite the expectations of more explosions and possibly bigger and more disastrous ones, workers moved in close to the stricken area. The sky was darkened by billowing black clouds of smoke. Occasional balls of flame shooting into the sky sent workermen scurrying for cover.

A blonde woman rushed by me and spoke to a company guard. He shook his head and said "no" to her. It was obvious what she had asked him. Some member of her family worked there and she wanted to know if that person was safe. Her eyes were red-rimmed from crying and the guard's answer had given her no comfort.

At the Medical Center an elderly Negro woman questioned a plant employee as to the safety of her husband. When told the man was safe, the woman seemed near collapse and hysteria.

Battleground? Yes. Due to something unknown at this time Tennessee Eastman resembled a battleground Tuesday. It was a battle of men trying to save their friends and fellow men.

The explosions, the blood, the death, the injured brought back vivid memories.

City Cleans Up
After Tragedy

It is the morning after the worst tragedy in the history of Kingsport and the city is cleaning up the debris.

In the eastern end of the city, which bore the brunt of Tuesday afternoon's tremendous explosion at Tennessee Eastman Company, untold thousands of dollars in damage was caused to private homes.

Everywhere you look makeshift windows have been installed from plywood and plastic. Some residents did not bother to cover gaping holes left by the shattered glass.

At Gibbons Lumber Co., and United Warehouse and Transfer on Eastman Road, huge plate glass windows were completely wrecked. The same was true at Cherokee Boat Co.

The entire front of Krogers on East Center Street was boarded up after the shattered glass fell to the pavement. Officials at the various firms said no estimate of the damage can be made at this time.

On Garden Drive, about a mile from the scene of the explosion, a six-inch long chunk of metal was hurled like a miniature meteor into the ground. It was red hot.

Also on Garden Drive, storm windows and doors were shattered, hurling glass into the living rooms of many families. One man reported his two children barely escaped being cut by the flying glass.

Doors and windows on Greenfield Ave. and Kenwood Road were also shattered.

A service station on Oakwood Drive look as if someone had tossed a bomb through the window.

At Pet Dairy on Konnarock Road, an entire ceiling in one building fell from the shock of the blast. Two men were working nearby but were not injured. Officials could give no accurate estimate of the damage.

Bob Ratcliff, General Manager of radio station WKPT, had grabbed some remote broadcast equipment and rushed to the explosion scene within minutes after it happened. He set up his equipment by the roadside, not wanting to be in the way of rescue workers and escaping workers, and relayed his eye-witness account back to Martin Karant at the radio station's studios, where it was fed out to a number of affiliated stations, and later, to the network.

Bob stayed on the scene until late that night, when it became clear that the work of rescue, clean up, and search would have to wait for daylight.

Chapter 27

The tragedy touched more lives than anyone has ever been able to number.

Statistically, local hospitals reported more than 200 injured in the explosion, and sadly, fifteen fatalities. But that does not count the devastating effect on family members, loved ones and friends.

No other occurrence in the area has affected practically every resident.

Following are the obituaries of the deceased:

Bernard C. Arnold

Funeral services were conducted Oct. 7 at the Carter-Clamon Chapel for B. C. Arnold, 50, of the Acid Division. The family home is at 249 DeLee Drive in Colonial Heights.

Mr. Arnold had been a resident of Kingsport for 17 years and had been employed at Eastman for 17 years.

He was a member of Ketron Memorial Methodist Church.

Survivors include his wife, Mrs. Peggy McCoy Arnold; one daughter, Mrs. (Eleanor A.) Jason Cox, Eastman; one son, Leslie Arnold, Eastman; his step-mother, Mrs. Belle Arnold, Max Meadows, Va.; three sisters, Mrs. Walter Bralley, Kingsport; Mrs. Hunter Colvin, Fernbank, Ala. and Mrs. Harold Wilkerson, Kingsport; two brothers, C. E.

Arnold, Eastman, and George S. Arnold, Kingsport; one grandson, several nieces and nephews, including Louise Bralley, a niece, and Bruce Bralley, a nephew, both at Eastman. Jason Cox, his son-in-law, is with Eastman.

J. D. Byington

J. D. Byington, 50, died Monday, Oct. 10 at Holston Valley Community Hospital.

Mr. Byington, whose home is on Route 1, Church Hill, had been with Eastman since 1947 and was in the S&M Division.

Funeral services were held Wednesday, Oct. 12 at the Morning Star Freewill Baptist Church.

Survivors include his wife, Mrs. Etta Sandidge Byington; two daughters, Shelby and Brenda, both of Church Hill; two sons, Eugene of Cincinnati, Ohio and Jimmie of Church Hill; three sisters, Mrs. John Bentley of Church Hill, Mrs. Paul Herron and Mrs. W. M. Gibbons, both of Kingsport; two brothers, Marshall of Church Hill and Marion of Kingsport; several nieces and nephews.

Dr. A. J. Chadwell

Dr. Andrew J. (Jack) Chadwell, Jr., 29, of the Acid Division, had worked as a research chemist. A native of Knox County, he had lived in Kingsport three years. His home was on South Holston Hills Road.

Funeral services were held Oct. 7 at Mann's Chapel, Knoxville.

Survivors include his wife, Mrs. Jane Mynatt Chadwell; one son, Andrew Grady Chadwell, both of Kingsport; one sister, Miss Carolyn Chadwell; one brother, Joseph Chadwell; his parents, Mr. and Mrs. A. J. Chadwell, Sr., all of Knoxville.

J. Carl Cochran

Funeral services for J. Carl Cochran, 53, Acid Division, were held Oct. 6 at the Broad Street Methodist Church. The family lives on Route 3, Kingsport, in Hemlock Park.

Cochran was born in Washington County. He lived in Fall Branch and had been with the Company 26 years.

Survivors include his wife, Mrs. Mabel Adams Cochran; one daughter, Mrs. John Odom, Smithtown, NY; one son, Dean Cochran, Holston Defense; five sisters, Mrs. Grace Chadwell, Kingsport; Mrs. Hubert Cloyd, Fall Branch; Mrs. Nancy Tarlton, Jonesboro and Mrs. Everett Baskett, Johnson City; one brother Paul Cochran, Johnson City and one grandson.

R. Carl Cox

R. Carl Cox, 59, of the Acid Division, died Monday, Oct. 10 at Holston Valley Community Hospital. Mr. Cox lived on Route 7, Jonesboro. He had been with the Company since May, 1940.

He is survived by his wife, Mrs. Sallie Cox; two daughters, Ruth Lisenby and Ruby Land, both in the Acetate Yarn Division, Kingsport; one son, Carl J. Cox, Jr., Jonesboro, Route 7; three brothers, A.F. Cox and R. L. Cox, an Eastman reitree, both of Kingsport and D. J. Cox, Jonesboro; two sisters, Mrs. C. F. Hilton and Mrs. R. L. Jobe of Jonesboro, two grandchildren. Both sons-in-law, George E. Land and Paul Lisenby, are with Eastman in the Research Laboratories and S&M Division, respectively. Two nephews, Charles F. Hilton and Kenneth E. Cox, are with the Company in the AY Division and ECPI, respectively.

Cornelius Y. Depew

Funeral services for Cornelius Y. Depew, 36, of Organic Chemicals were held Oct. 8, in the Gate City Methodist Church. The Rev. Ray P. Hargraves and the Rev. H. C. Camper were in charge. Burial followed in the Holston View Cemetery. The family lives on Route 3, Church Hill.

Mr. Depew had been with the company over 11 years. He was a member of the American Legion.

Survivors include his wife, Edna Myers Depew; three daughters, Elizabeth Ann, Ronda Sue and Vada Lee; one son Charles, all of Church Hill; his parents, Mr. and Mrs. Roy L. Depew, Hiltons, Va.; five sisters, Mrs. Fred Clark, Mrs. Harold Clark, Mrs. Harry Driscal and Miss Connie Depew, all of Hiltons; Mrs. H. D. Curtis, Weber City; four brothers, Roy L. Depew, Jr., Gate City; Alvin Depew, Vinnia, Va.; Orville and Bobby Depew, both of Hiltons.

Mr. Depew's father, Roy L. Depew, is with Eastman.

Usif Haney

Usif Haney, 45, was chemist in charge of the Aniline Plant in the Organic Chemicals Division. A graduate of Michigan State University, he joined the Company in June, 1940.

Survivors include his wife, Mrs. Eloise Pomeroy Haney; two sons, Bruce and Kevin, Kingsport; four sisters, Mrs. Kelly Goad, Mrs. J. B. Windle, and Miss Neshma Haney, all of Kingsport and Mrs. G. T. McGuire, Jr., Atlanta, Ga.; one brother, Major Shaheen Haney, stationed in North Carolina. J. B. Windle, of Eastman, is a brother-in-law.

I. D. Mullins

Funeral services for I. D. Mullins, 39, of the Acid Division, were held October 7, in the Goshen Valley Methodist Church. Mr. Mullins had been with the

Company since Oct., 1940. He lived at 401 Chadwell Road in Kingsport.

He is survived by his wife, Mrs. Irene Jones Mullins, 401 Chadwell Road; one son, Ivan David Mullins; five sisters, Kate Mullins, Mrs. Vesta Gilbert, Mrs. Ellen Skelton, Mrs. Linie Patterson and Mrs. Irene Buchanan, all of Church Hill; two brothers, Pershing, of Eastman and Orr Mullins, Church Hill.

Manze Powers

Manze Powers, 50, of the Shops and Maintenance Division, was buried Oct. 8, in the cemetery adjoining the Eastern Star Baptist Church in Fordtown.

Mr. Powers lived near Fall Branch, and had been with the Company nearly 17 years.

He is survived by his wife, Mrs. Mary Leona Hite Powers; three daughters, Mrs. Reba Blakely, New Lebanon, Ohio; Mrs. Betty Willis, Jonesboro and Pauline Powers, Kingsport; four sons, Sgt. Robert E. Powers, US Army in Germany; Manze Powers, Jr., Jonesboro; Jimmy Lee and Harry W. Powers, Kingsport; his father, C. W. Powers, Jonesboro; four sisters, Mrs. Elena Willis, Kingsport; Mrs. Maxie McCrary, Jonesboro; Mrs. Lonnie Addison, New Ridgefields, Ohio; three brothers, Ross C. Powers, Kingsport; Guy M. Powers, Jonesboro and Oscar F. Powers, Jonesboro.

Ed O. Repass

Ed O. Repass, 51 of Stores & Warehousing, was buried in Oak Hill Cemetery following funeral services Oct. 7 in the Gate City Methodist Church.

Survivors include his wife, Lucille Larkey Repass, Hiltons, Va.; two daughters, Mrs. Paul Bright, Hiltons and Miss Norma J. Repass, Radford, Va.; two sons, Edward O.

Repass II, and Barton L. Repass, both of Hiltons; three sisters Mrs. O. O. Crowell, Pulaski, Va.; Mrs. B. L. Musser, Rural Retreat, Va.; and Mrs. T. C. Weeks, Detroit, Mich.; three brothers, R. M. Repass, Kingsport; Luther Repass, Dublin, Va.; and Oscar Repass, Cocoa, Fla.

James W. (Ott) Sage, Jr.

Funeral services for James W. Sage, Jr. were conducted Oct. 7 at Sunnyside Baptist Church. Burial was in East Lawn Memorial Park. Mr. Sage was 28 years old and had been with the Company since July, 1953. He was in the Acid Division. His home was in the Bridwell Heights Addition at Indian Springs.

Survivors include his wife, Mrs. Peggy Jolene Campbell Sage; one daughter, Kimberly Jo; one son, James William Sage III, all of Indian Springs; his parents, Mr. and Mrs. James William Sage, Sr., Kingsport; four sisters, Mrs. Louise Barrett, Mrs. Helen Thornburg, Miss Juanita Sage and Miss Bobbie Jean Sage, all of Kingsport; two brothers, Garland Sage of Sandusky, Ohio and Frank Sage of Kingsport.

Jimmie W. Sanders

The funeral for Jimmie W. Sanders, 27, of the Office Services Department, was held Oct. 7 at Wheeler's Methodist Church. The Rev. Wayne Cummings and the Rev. Virgil Anderson were in charge. Burial was in Gunnings Cemetery. Mr. Sanders had lived on Route 3, Blountville.

Survivors include his wife, Mrs. Mary Ann Hodges Sanders, two sons, Sammy and Andy Sanders; his parents, Frank H. and Anna Lee Click Sanders; all of Holston Institute; two sisters, Mrs. A. B. Burleson, Huntsville, Ala.; Mrs. J. E. Johnson, Chapel Hill, NC; one brother,

Howard L. Sanders, Holston Institute. His father-in-law is Lawrence Hodges of Eastman.

Jess Ray Shell

Jess Ray Shell, 35, of the Organic Chemicals Division, was buried in the East Lawn Memorial Park Cemetery Oct. 7 following funeral services at the Lynn Garden Evangelical Methodist Church.

Survivors include his wife, Helen Shell; one son, Jess Ray Shell III, three sisters, Mrs. E. J. Falin, Gate City; Mrs. Ray Falin, Oak Ridge, and Mrs. Tommy King, Fort Bragg, NC; one brother, James R. Kilgore, Kingsport; his mother, Mrs. Josephine Kilgore; and step-father, Richard Kilgore of Eastman.

John W. Squibb

John W. Squibb, 44, of the Organic Chemicals Division, had been with the Company since Jan. 1942. Funeral services were held Oct. 7 in the Leesburg Presbyterian Church in Leesburg, Tenn.

Survivors include his wife, Mrs. Marie Fleenor Squibb; one daughter Rebekah; one brother, Charles Squibb, Tavores, Fla.; and one sister, Lucy Waddle, Greeneville.

Arthur H. Stevens

Funeral services for Arthur H. Stevens, 44, of Route 1, Indian Springs, were conducted Oct. 6 in the Cedar View Methodist Church by the Rev. W. R. Dillon and burial was in the East Lawn Memorial Park.

Mr. Stevens was born in Washington County, Va. and had been a resident of Sullivan County for the past 30 years.

Survivors include his wife, Mrs. Laura Mae Stevens; one daughter, Susan; two sons, Darryl and David, all of Indian

Springs; one sister, Mrs. Julian Coffey, Indian Springs; three brothers, Carmel and Phillip, both of Eastman and Herman Stevens of Kingsport; his mother, Mrs. Pearl Stevens, Indian Springs. Shields Price, of Eastman, is his father-in-law.

Chapter 28

Harold Manis was an instrument tech at Eastman, and had been servicing and checking instruments in the Aniline Plant since it was built in 1956-57.

It was rumored that "Dr." Harold Von Bramer, who had been in charge of that particular manufacturing chemical process had refused to allow such a plant to be built while he was in charge. Reportedly, he had maintained that the process was too dangerous, it was said, believing that the hot nitric acid mixed with benzene went through a molecular structure that was very close to nitroglycerine.

A chemical genius, Harold Von Bramer had been brought to Eastman in the early days of the plant from New Jersey where he had developed chemical processes required by the manufacturing plant.

Designers of the new plant, however, chose to disregard those earlier warnings, paying close attention instead to what they considered more modern safety features.

The initial Aniline Plant start up, three years before the fateful day of the explosion, had lasted only about a week. Suddenly, leaks were discovered everywhere, which caused an immediate shut down. Manis was involved with the valves that were used.

When the valves were taken apart, the insides looked very like porous balsa wood. That was also true of the pump bodies and piping that had been made of stainless steel. The leaks, caused by erosion, were mainly in the area of the plant where the nitric and benzene were being mixed.

The plant Machine Shop remade valve bodies, stems, seats, pump bodies and pipes of Titanium. Because this all happened during the "maiden voyage" of the plant, production problems seem to have been solved, and the work continued for three years.

Following that initial "shake down" operation, the plant was always started up at night when the least number of workers would be present.

The control room, overlooking the Aniline Plant through a large plate glass window, was situated about 40 yards away.

In late September 1960, the Aniline Plant had been shut down for maintenance. Everything was checked and tested. NO one seemed to be in a hurry to restart the plant, and all the instruments were checked and rechecked.

Manis and other Instrument Techs had been in the building for most of the past two weeks.

On October 4, 1960, the plant was started up at about 11:00 a.m., the first time a daytime start up had occurred.

About 4:15, Manis asked Usif Haney, who was in charge of the building, if he needed the Techs to stay over after hours.

Haney leaned against one of the handrails and said no.

"Go on home," he told Manis. "If I need you, I will call you."

There was to be a meeting of the Instrument Society of America that night, and Manis wanted to attend, so he left the plant a few minutes early in order to do some work at home before coming back to the Eastman for the meeting.

Driving home, he was in his car at a traffic light, gazing toward a local drug store when the explosion occurred.

"A lady was walking out of the door at the drug store and had only taken a couple of steps when the plate glass window popped out just behind her. My car also shook", he recalled.

Manis turned his car around and drove back to the hill overlooking Eastman from the Borden Mills, confirming his suspicion that it was the Aniline plant.

Manis' memory of the following events was reported in the "DBer Newsletter" in 2005.

"There was continuous noise that lasted into the night, overhead pipelines, running next to the building had been broken and caught on fire. They threw out a flame about 25 to 30 yards. It looked like a gigantic blowtorch. This was the hydrogen from the storage tanks. In order to empty the tanks, they elected to allow the gases to keep burning. They also knew the danger of their "blowing". There were small explosions on into the night in other buildings. Fires had started and fifty-five gallon drums of different types of chemicals got hot enough to explode.

"After calling my family to let them know I was all right, I called Martin Karant at WKPT (radio) to let them know what had happened. Until I called, they thought that the explosion was at the Blue Ridge Glass Plant or Holston Defense Area A.

"I found a fellow worker that was in his car, a Henry J. He had purchased a pair of fog lights from the operator in the control room of the Aniline Plant who was killed in the blast. My friend, G.W., was bent over, putting the fog lights under the passenger's seat when the blast came. He said his doors opened and closed and a piece of pipe about a foot long came through the passenger window hitting the brace between the front and rear seat. Had he been sitting upright, it would have hit him in the head.

"Another fellow worker was walking through the Clock station with a friend. His friend had just exited the door and was in the open and was killed.

"Carl Cochrane was in the street just below Building 207 and was killed by flying material from the blast.

"A pick up truck was pinned to the ground by a H-beam near the Long Island Bridge. The beam slammed down between the cab, the bed and the running board. A 300 gallon tank wound up under the Island Bridge."

Manis' hard hat been left on top of a chart recorder on a work bench. A piece of cast iron came through the roof and hit the hat and the recorder, then bounced off a wall cabinet.

About two years passed before Manis' supervisor asked him if he would go into the control room for the Aniline Plant and remove four instruments needed for another project. The control room operator had been killed in the explosion and the room had been boarded up and padlocked since the explosion.

"Because I worked there, Manis said, "I was familiar with what the readings on the charts were to be. I didn't see any abnormal recordings until that moment when all the recorders went to "0" at 4:43 p.m."

The plant was never rebuilt. What happened? Nobody knows, not even today. The only men who might possibly have known were the two men blown to bits in the explosion. And they may not have known either.

Chapter 29

At the local hospital, the sudden unexpected emergency situation would soon tax both staff and equipment to absolute limits.

October 4, 1960 had been a beautiful autumn day, and Dr. Jim Brown was relaxed and smiling when he walked out of his office in the Medical Arts Building on Revere Street in Kingsport. The afternoon sun's warm glow felt good on his face.

Because the weather was so pleasant, Dr. Brown decided to leave his car in the parking lot and walk the few yards to the Hospital where he would check on patients that had been admitted.

The peaceful walk would be the last bit of relaxation he would enjoy for many hours to come.

The account of Dr. Jim Brown

October 4, 1960 was a fine autumn day, and Jim Brown smiled as he stepped outside of his Medical Arts Building office on Ravine Street in Kingsport, Tennessee and felt the warm afternoon sun on his face.

As president of the Holston Valley Community Hospital Medical Staff, Dr. Brown had a busy schedule.

His private practice as an Internist required considerable time, and the additional responsibilities of the hospital duties added more work hours, taking away time from his wife and family.

His three daughters were growing up, and he sometimes envied those men who seemed to have ample time for all sorts of activities with their children.

That morning, Dr. Brown had parked his car in the hospital parking lot, and now, as he walked toward the large brick facility, he decided to leave the car where it was and pace the short distance to his destination.

Although he was now firmly rooted in Kingsport and East Tennessee, a few years earlier, Jim Brown had not had any intention of ever locating in the area.

After his Medical School training; three additional years study in Louisville to obtain more knowledge of internal medicine, and duty with the US Navy, Dr. Brown was ready to settle down in a regular practice that would enable him to support his family and reward him with the satisfaction of being the healer he longed to become.

He had fulfilled those dreams and ambitions in Kingsport, and adopted the city firmly as his "chosen" hometown.

Born in a small town in Mississippi, his dream had been to become a successful doctor in his home state or in that general area, and he had even taken a job with an older doctor in a small Mississippi town for a while; just after his release from service with the US Navy.

It had been in Memphis, Tennessee, that he met the girl he later married, Lil Von Bramer, of Kingsport. Lil was there taking a nursing course, and before long they were engaged.

But military duty called first, so Jim became a Navy Doctor.

With the permission of his skipper, he was able to take a leave and come to Kingsport to marry Lil, on May 4, 1946.

The Navy at that time was decommissioning a number of Mine Sweepers near Houston, Texas. The ships were taken up the Sabin River there, anchored, and "put in moth balls".

Guns were oiled and repairs were made as needed and some "polyester stuff" was used to cover sensitive equipment. There was a little town up river from Houston, where Dr. Jim and his bride rented a small house to live in. They often fished the river during their stay there.

Although it seemed at the time that the ships might never be used again, the Korean Conflict came soon afterwards, and the Mine Sweepers were put back into service.

In the meantime, Jim and Lil's first daughter was born, and the young new father began to think more seriously about his future both as a family man and as a physician.

What he was looking for was a place with opportunity for a young doctor, where he could set up practice following his discharge from the Navy.

Frequently, he and Lil would use his "leave time" from the Navy going to investigate the possibilities of areas in Mississippi and all over the South, never considering Kingsport at all.

It was Lil's mother who made Jim a Kingsporter, and in an unexpected way.

Jim and Lil had left their daughter with her grandparents while they made a quick trip to check out possibilities of another town.

That one did not pan out either.

Hearing discouraging reports from former classmates in that area, Jim realized that the weary search would have to continue.

Returning to the Von Bramer home in Kingsport, to pick up their little girl who had been left with her grandmother, they had discussed how difficult it was to find a good location before retiring to bed for the night.

The following morning, when Jim awakened, he found two applications for Holston Valley Hospital on the bed, ready to fill out and submit.

Not only that, but both applications had already been signed by local doctors, Reed and Bureum, recommending that Jim Brown be accepted to the hospital staff, a required necessity for admittance at that time. His mother-in-law had obtained the forms and the signatures during the previous night, a gentle hint that Jim should consider Kingsport as a future home.

Before long, he was establishing a practice in Kingsport. A few months later, their second daughter was born.

Within a year or two after establishing his practice of Internal Medicine, Jim was recalled to active duty in the Navy.

A friend heard of his plight and offered some sound advice.

"You ought to go to Washington and tell them that you are just getting started and that your wife is having her third baby," the friend said.

That was certainly true enough, so Jim flew up to Washington and took a taxi to the Naval building. It was early morning when he got there, and he was able to go right in and see the officer in charge.

When the officer heard his story, he said "Well, I guess East Tennessee needs you worse than we do," and released him from duty.

As the years passed by Dr. Brown's practice grew and he continued involvement with the Holston Valley Hospital, at last becoming President of the Medical Staff.

On that fateful afternoon of the Eastman explosion, Dr. Brown had just arrived at the hospital doorway when the sound of a tremendous blast rent the air and the concrete walkway beneath his feet seemed to shake.

Realizing that some drastic event had taken place, the physician immediately ran inside the hospital and took the elevator to the sixth floor, the highest peak of the building.

As soon as the elevator doors opened, Dr. Brown rushed to a nearby window and gazed out, his eyes searching the horizon.

In the distance, he could see a large cloud of smoke rising in the direction of the Tennessee Eastman Chemical plant, and knew instinctively that terrible trouble was just moments away.

Calling a quick meeting of any medical staff doctors who happened to be in the hospital at the time, Dr. Brown told them his conclusions and immediately adopted the emergency plan that had been prepared only weeks earlier.

The Senior Nurse who was in charge on that floor, Mrs. Jim Dennis, was sent, along with Dr. Kenneth Kiesau, to the front of the hospital to await arriving ambulances and triage the injury victims.

Dr. Kiesau was experienced in making snap decisions about which wounded was in most need of immediate treatment. He had done this type of work in the service, overseas, very near the front lines.

There, he had been responsible for meeting ambulances coming in and for sending the wounded to the right places for treatment, and he had volunteered to do that same duty on the Emergency Team.

Dr. Duckwall, a talented local surgeon, had forseen the need of an emergency plan following a very stressful experience of his own.

A horrifying bus wreck near Morristown had injured many persons. Dr. Duckwall was the surgical doctor on call the night of the wreck and all the seriously injured patients had been brought to Holston Valley for him to treat. He had thirty patients at the same time, all needing immediate help.

With the able assistance of talented nurses he had been able to take care of the emergency, but realized the desperate need of a plan of action for just such situations in the future.

At a medical meeting, he outlined the problem and made suggestions, and the entire staff agreed. They selected committees and doctors volunteered to write up their own recommendations, which were submitted to Dr. Brown for consideration.

Thus a plan for emergency situations was created, and was in place when needed.

At that time there were no emergency room doctors, no physicians who specialized in treating emergency patients.

All doctors on the staff agreed to take turns at being in charge of the emergency room at a specific time, so that it would be ready 24 hours a day, seven days a week.

It soon become apparent that the explosion had occured at the Eastman plant, but no one had any idea of how extensive it may have been.

As the ambulances began to arrive with injured victims, doctors began to realize that they were up against a real problem.

The hospital had an emergency room, of course, and some of the doctors were stationed there to treat people who were bleeding with lesions or other more minor injuries.

Those persons with deeper and more severe wounds were sent to the Surgical Suite area, where a few beds were available.

A good many persons had lacerations from glass that had been blown out of windows and shattered and those individuals who needed more extensive surgery were put back in what was called the "Intensive Care" unit.

Just a few years earlier, there had been nothing in that area except Iron Lungs, used to treat Polio patients who could not breathe, but since the Salk Vaccine had been successful in eliminating most Polio cases, the Iron Lungs were no longer needed and had been removed changing the space into its current use.

Many of the severely injured who arrived were put on stretchers or beds that had been rolled down to the lobby area. They were wrapped in blankets and taken to the Surgical Suite. Trying to be as quick as possible, nurses did not take time to remove the injured person's street clothes, but merely wrapped them in blankets to await being taken to surgery.

Before long, one of the physicians noticed that some patients' lips and fingernails were getting a blue tinge of color.

Conferring with other doctors, Jim Brown concluded that patients were suffering from a severe cyanosis, and puzzled over it cause.

None of the physicians on hand had any knowledge of the chemicals that may have been involved, and how to treat reactions to them. Although there were many volunteers including two or three doctors from Bristol and a total force of more than a hundred by that time, none of them were familiar with the reactions that might have been caused by substances spread by the explosion.

Patients wrapped in blankets began to have difficulty breathing and Dr. Brown and others kept the telephone lines busy calling other area hospitals seeking information and advice.

At last, a person in the Medical Department at Eastman was located, and was able to explain that the blue tinge lips and fingernails probably meant toxic reaction to Aniline dye, a reaction commonly called "Blue Lip" by dye plant workers.

"It closes up the pores in the skin," the spokesman said, "and it can cause death."

"How do we treat it?" the doctor asked.

"Well..." the spokesman hesitated. "You better call Rochester and ask them. There is not any of the Medical staff here at this time and I just don't know."

The Rochester NY number was given and called immediately, and a treatment was recommended, Methylene Blue, of a certain type to be made up, and given intravenously.

Patients who had been splashed with the dye in the explosion were lying in soaked clothing, wrapped in blankets, and absorbing the dye through their skin!

There was an additional flurry of activity as the blankets were taken off and discarded, clothing removed, bodies washed down, and rewrapped in blankets to await further treatment.

The Hospital Pharmacy did not have any of the Methylene Blue needed for the treatment, and neither did any area hospitals or pharmacies.

Rochester was called again.

"We will send some on the very next plane that leaves here," the voice promised.

"But be sure you take those blankets off those people and wash them down good. You will have the Methylene Blue in a few hours."

Immediately, the patients who had been wrapped in blankets were checked. The blankets were removed, the bodies washed down, and clean hospital gowns and bedding added.

A worried Medical Staff continued to work through the night, setting broken bones, stitching up multiple cuts, and treating other injuries.

Dr. Brown worked through the night, along with the entire staff of medical assistants, physicians, and volunteers.

By morning, the patients who had shown blue tinges to fingernails and lips were considerably better, their toxins beginning to dissipate.

Bill Shaw, one of Dr. Brown's friends, was badly lacerated from broken glass. Dr. Sheldon Reed was assigned to do surgery on his face.

"Are you going to put me to sleep before you sew these cuts up?" Shaw asked. "You are, aren't you?"

"Well," Dr. Reed replied, "we haven't decided yet."

As it turned out, anesthetizing the patient was not necessary. Novocaine was put in to all the cuts, and Shaw's face was sewn up with such skill that after he healed, no scaring at all was visible.

With more than a hundred medical personnel on the emergency staff, patients were treated promptly and efficiently, but it was a long, and tedious, worrisome night.

Physicians, surgeons and nurses did remarkable and heroic work, saving lives and treating injuries.

Although there were many persons who deserved credit for the desperate work done that night, and all of them deserved praise for a job well done, the foresight of Dr. Duckwall, who had originated the idea and had insisted that the hospital establish an emergency plan, may have been more responsible for success than any other.

And it may have been one of his last great achievements in his profession.

"Not long afterward, Dr. Duckwall was up on the floor, waiting to do an operation, when he began to suffer chest pain." Dr. Brown recalls.

"He went back out to lay down, and he died right up there on the floor."

Hopefully, there will never again be such a night and such a sudden, unexpected emergency.

But if such a thing occurs, local medical care providers will be ready.

Conclusion

There are hundreds, perhaps even thousands, of personal memories and reactions yet lodged in the minds of those who remember the tragic explosion. In this work, we have tried to record a sampling of the thoughts, reactions and feelings of some of them.

In almost all the memories we have gathered, the prevailing concern was not for the individual but for others.

Worry, fear and anxiety certainly were a full part of the moments and hours of that tragic day, but those emotions were for friends and loved ones rather than for themselves. Such reactions make us proud of our town and our people, and we are grateful that the Kingsport community takes, in time of stress and disaster, the higher plain rather than basic self-interest.

So long as memory remains, the Eastman explosion will be a vivid and fearful picture in the minds of many. The tragic demise of fifteen good men make it one of the saddest times in East Tennessee's history.

www.ingramcontent.com/pod-product-compliance
Lightning Source LLC
Chambersburg PA
CBHW060346100426
42812CB00003B/1142